FLIGHTS OF THE TINGMISSARTOQ

C.A.L. 1938

LISTEN! THE WIND

By the same author

NORTH TO THE ORIENT

Listen! the Wind

BY ANNE MORROW LINDBERGH

WITH FOREWORD AND MAP DRAWINGS BY

CHARLES A. LINDBERGH

HARCOURT, BRACE AND COMPANY, NEW YORK

Fourth printing, November, 1938

Acknowledgment is made to the *National Geographic Magazine* for permission to reprint certain paragraphs from "Flying Around the North Atlantic" by Anne Morrow Lindbergh.

PRINTED IN THE UNITED STATES OF AMERICA
Typography by Robert Josephy

FOREWORD

BY CHARLES A. LINDBERGH

"LISTEN! THE WIND" is the story of a survey flight around the North Atlantic Ocean
in 1933. It is a true and accurate account of
various incidents which occurred in flying from
Africa to South America. The purpose of the
flight was to study the air-routes between America
and Europe. At that time, the air-routes of the
world were entering their final stage of develop-
ment. The countries had already been crossed
and the continents connected. It remained only
for the oceans to be spanned. Their great over-
water distances constituted the last major barrier
to the commerce of the air.

The North Atlantic is the most important, and
also the most difficult to fly, of all the oceans
crossed by the trade routes of men. Distance and
climate have combined to place obstacles in the
path of those who wish to travel over it. Where
the distance is short, the climate is severe, as in the
north; while in the south, great distances counter-
act the advantages of a milder season. There are
three natural air-routes across the North Atlantic.

v

They may be designated as the "Greenland Route" in the north, the "Azores Route" in the south, and the "Great Circle Route" in the center. We were to survey them all.

Our flight began at New York in July, and after following the "Great Circle Route" to Newfoundland, turned north along the coast of Labrador. We crossed to Europe over the "Northern Route," making our first continental landing at Copenhagen. The following weeks were spent in the countries of Europe, and in flights along the coasts of Norway, Scotland, Ireland, Spain, and Portugal.

We reached the Azores too late in the year to fly to Newfoundland or Bermuda with the facilities which then existed. The risk would have been unnecessarily great. So, after a few days in these islands, we set our course south to Africa and the less difficult route which passes over the equator to South America. *Listen! the Wind* is written about our homeward trip, or rather that portion of it which lay between Africa and South America. It describes the people we met and the problems we encountered in making a long over-water flight without advance organization and with a plane originally constructed for continental flying.

Our plane, the *Tingmissartoq* [1] was designed

[1] Named in Greenland for the Eskimo cry when a plane is sighted—"Tingmissartoq" (the one who flies like a big bird).

in 1929 for survey flying over continental routes. As a landplane, in 1930, it had broken the transcontinental record between California and New York. In 1931, the wheels were replaced with pontoons for a flight over the Arctic route to the Orient. Two years later, a more powerful engine was installed, and the plane equipped for our trip over the air-routes of the Atlantic.

It was necessary to be as independent as possible of outside assistance. In 1933, there were no facilities for aircraft at most of the places where we landed. In fact we considered ourselves fortunate when we found a good anchorage and a well-placed buoy to moor to. We followed no predetermined route, and the time we spent in each place depended upon the conditions we encountered and the interest we found in that area. We often reached our destination without advance information about landing conditions. If they were bad, as at Madeira, we continued on to some other location. We never took off without having alternate destinations within our range.

This type of flying necessitated unusual reserves, both in fuel and in emergency equipment. On most flights our plane was heavily overloaded when measured by conventional standards. Our safety lay not in dogmatic formulas of performance and structure, but in the proper balance of constantly changing factors. Sometimes safety lay

in a quick take-off, as among the icebergs at
Angmagssalik; sometimes in a long range, as for
our flight across the Atlantic to Brazil. And
always in extra rations and emergency equipment.

We carried two complete and independent
radio sets, one of which was waterproof and fitted
into a rubber sailboat. We traded part of our
plane's performance for additional days of food
and water, for guns, for a bug-proof tent, and for
all the many items which are needed when an
emergency arises.

As a result, we had the best radio communication ever obtained in many of the areas we flew
over. A forced landing, either on land or at sea,
would have left us in a position to live, to travel,
and to communicate. And in the thirty thousand
miles of our flight we were never without an
adequate reserve of fuel in our tanks.

We encountered the main disadvantage from
our heavy load in taking off. To take off with
full tanks, we needed a good wind and a long
stretch of sheltered water.

Our flight lasted for nearly six months. This
book covers only ten days of that time. It is about
a period in aviation which is now gone, but which
was probably more interesting than any the future will bring. As time passes, the perfection of
machinery tends to insulate man from contact

FOREWORD ix

with the elements in which he lives. The "strato-sphere" planes of the future will cross the ocean without any sense of the water below. Like a train tunneling through a mountain, they will be aloof from both the problems and the beauty of the earth's surface. Only the vibration from the en-gines will impress the senses of the traveler with his movement through the air. Wind and heat and moonlight take-offs will be of no concern to the transatlantic passenger. His only contact with these elements will lie in accounts such as this book contains.

CONTENTS

PART 1

SANTIAGO

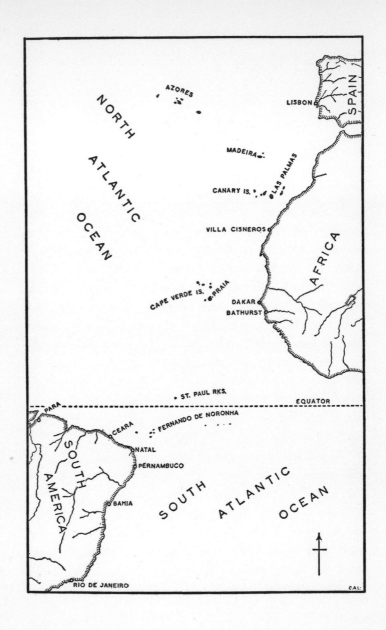

CHAPTER I

TAIL WIND

TAIL WIND—I looked down over the side of the plane at the long white streaks in the water below us. White streamers, irregular as raveled threads and yet all pointing in one direction, all paralleling the course of the plane from the coast of Africa southwest to the Cape Verde Islands. The wind had helped us ever since we left the Azores; pushing behind our backs, roaring at our heels, whistling in the cowlings; carrying us along in its stream as a boat is carried on its last stretch home, going "before the wind" with the sail full out, not making any effort of its own, being wafted along on a great tide, swiftly and easily.

So we had come from Spain. Last night outside the tents of the Moors on that dry spit of desert Africa; the night before at Las Palmas in the Canary Islands, among the bazaars and shops, the docks and markets of that old crossroad of the east and west. One jump back from Las Palmas and we had been at the Azores, stepping stones in the Atlantic. One jump before that, Lisbon.

3

So we had come by giant strides: Horta, Ponta
Delgada, Las Palmas, Rio de Oro. And always
the wind filling up our cups to overflowing, giving us a little more time, a little more fuel than
we expected. The wind—which one can never
count on, which sometimes, bearing down on one
wing or on another, lures one imperceptibly out
of one's course. Or, towering in one's face, makes
the flight a long uphill climb, draining away the
precious daylight, devouring the fuel. This wind,
usually so perverse, uncontrollable, and fickle, had
been ours for two thousand miles. Miraculously,
it had been ours to count upon as though, like the
old story of Odysseus, some god had imprisoned in
a bag of ox's skin all opposing winds, leaving free
only that one which was to take us home.

For we were on our way home. Our survey
flight of the North Atlantic was over. A summer
in Greenland and Iceland, an early fall in the
mists and rains of Europe. Copenhagen, Sta-
vanger, Southampton, the coasts of Scotland and
Ireland, Spain and Portugal, the Azores—all jumping-off places for new routes to America—had
been touched and passed. Then down the coast
of Africa (leaving the cold and rain behind,
breaking out of the clouds into clear skies, a hot
sun, and prevailing winds) for our last lap across
the Atlantic.

It was a long jump, that last one, sixteen hundred miles from the Cape Verde Islands to the coast of South America. But that one flight, that sustained stretch of twelve hours over the ocean, would put us out of one hemisphere and into another. We would be in America. How soon? Day after tomorrow night, I wondered, would that gigantic step be behind us? A week from today where would we be, I mused, looking down at those innumerable little white ripples in a dazzling sea. Somewhere on the coast of South America, on a regular airline, over territory we had crossed before? Paramaribo—Georgetown—Trinidad—all familiar names, familiar places—on our way home.

It seemed unbelievable. And yet no miracle would surprise me today, I felt, sitting on the top of the sky, the wind at our backs, the horizon opening up clear and void before us—dazzlingly clear, the blue arch burned white by the brilliance of the sun. With the great strides of the summer's flight behind us, and the wide limitless sky ahead, there was no end to our powers. Yesterday we had passed Europe; today we touched Africa; tomorrow we would be in America.

Only one step more, and our jumping-off place in the Cape Verde Islands was ahead of us. These bare, brown, broken-off scraps of the African continent are two hundred miles nearer to South America than the closest part of Africa. It is over eighteen hundred miles from Dakar, on the bulge of Africa, to Natal on the bulge of South America. But from Santiago, a small island in the Cape Verde group, to Natal is only about sixteen hundred. The difference between sixteen hundred and eighteen hundred miles was, for our plane, a difference between having a good fuel reserve and having barely enough to make the flight in safety; between making a normal cruising speed and having to throttle down to a much slower speed in order to conserve gasoline; between a daylight flight and one which encroached upon darkness. It was the difference, in fact, between an easy flight and a difficult one.

So it was with great satisfaction, earlier in the summer, that my husband, studying the charts of the Atlantic, measuring distances, looking up harbors, decided that we should be able to take off from a southern island of the Cape Verde group. Although the charts showed no land-locked harbor, Porto Praia seemed fairly well sheltered from the prevailing wind. And, most encouraging of all, it had a seaplane base for the French trans-atlantic service. Refueling arrangements had been made; our course laid out; our radio schedules planned with the South American stations. All that remained for us was to land at Porto Praia, to refuel, to set out, and then—with a tail wind— with a tail wind . . .

CHAPTER II

COULD WE LAND?

M Y husband rocked the plane to attract my
attention; then passed back a message for
me to send out by radio.

"POSITION   13:00 GMT
        17° 40′ N
        20° 40′ W
    BOAVISTA SIGHTED [Why, yes, there they were
    —soft gray bumps on the horizon ahead—the
    Cape Verde Islands.] WILL LAND PORTO PRAIA
    ABOUT 15:00."

Only two hours more, and it was just noon.
Tail wind, of course—

The islands at first looked like most islands
seen at a distance, nebulous, soft and gray, as
though made of the same substance as the ocean;
a row of waves a little higher than the neighbor-
ing waves, caught at their crests momentarily,
soon to sink down among their equals again. But
gradually they took a more definite shape. The
crests of the waves became fixed, their shapes
asymmetrical. Their color, too, separated from

the sea, hardened into a darker gray, lost its light atmospheric quality.

As we came nearer we could see they were not round knobs of equal height protruding evenly from the sea. Light clouds, which were not visible before, hovered over the islands and covered some of the volcanic peaks, making them appear to be of the same height. Their shores too, far from sloping gently into the ocean, were cut up, ragged and irregular, scattered with rocks and ledges as though indicating a constant struggle with the elements around them. Here a jagged promontory had succeeded in defending itself against the waves, still furiously pounding in white froth at its feet. But there the sea had encroached upon the land, driving it back into a shallow harbor, a meek curve.

The whole of Santiago presented this strangely scalloped profile, as though great bites had been taken out of a once perfectly rounded island. The interior of the island, rising to a volcanic point, looked weather-beaten, browned by the sun, bare and dry, cut up here and there by great green cracks in its rough surface, barrancas washed by tropical rains, in which were huddled small clumps of trees.

It was not desert like the coast of Africa behind us, I thought, looking at the gorges softened by gray-green trees, and the even lines of cultivation in some of the valleys. It was not jungle like the coasts of South America ahead of us. It was unrelated to any country I could remember. These islands—what were they like? I groped in my mind for something comparable. They were just islands, suspended in the Atlantic, lost islands, jumping-off places.

Our jumping-off place at least, it would be. Hadn't we picked it out of the clear outlines of a chart, putting a finger on the very harbor now below us, looking down at the contours like gods surveying the world? There, we had said, we will land there, refuel, and take off on this straight line for South America. Like gods still we were, looking down from our great height at the scalloped shore line, the minute ripples glistening far below, the toy boats bobbing in the water, the little stone houses, yellow and pink, bordering like pebbles the half-moon harbor of Porto Praia. There was our destination below us. Our fuel was in one of those pink pebbles.

Leaving our Olympian heights we began to circle down, the engine breathing more easily in a glide, the air whistling in the cowlings. Praia was a good-sized town. There were streets going down to the water's edge but most of the town was set back on a rise above the harbor. One could pick out the center square with evenly placed trees making a green border. The harbor, although large, was not sheltered; great waves were coming right up the beach. Those tiny ripples I had seen from above were giant rollers. No wonder the boats were bobbing about.

Well, I thought, of course there was quite a strong wind today. Rough air, too. The plane bucked like a horse as we passed over the valley, circled the town, and turned out to sea again. Very bumpy. Perhaps my picture was wrong. Perhaps we were not riding the wind like omnipotent gods. Perhaps, instead, our plane was a tiny sliver of bark, tossed this way and that on the choppy surface of a great unruly sea of air.

The plane, also, seemed to me endowed with passions and a will of its own. It would tear around one curve like a runaway horse, the bit in its teeth; and then stubbornly refuse to take the opposite one, holding off as long as it could, headstrong and hard-mouthed. Round and round the harbor of Porto Praia we went, holding back against the swift turns and banking into the slow ones; watching the half-moon rim of surf below us climb up a pebbly beach and then retreat slowly to the sea; watching the long rollers ride like shadows over the water, darken, accumulate, and disappear in foam against the land, with more following, always more behind, even lines darkening, advancing, closing in, unchecked from the open sea.

We could never land there, not today anyway, with that wind. Perhaps on a calm day— My husband opened the throttle. We roared up from the bay and headed down the coast. Another harbor perhaps, a more sheltered cove—

In a minute or two, we came upon a tiny opening in the rocky coast where there was a small settlement; a concrete pier, a hangar, several shacks, and two radio towers—the French transatlantic base. The narrow tongue of water, between two rocky points, was not large enough to land in, but would offer good protection from the wind, at least while it was in that direction. We could land outside and anchor there for the night. Besides, how comforting to see the broad roof and great open door of a modern hangar, the concrete pier with a big derrick at its edge, the neat white-painted houses and two tall radio towers. Here was the world of Aviation. Here was efficiency; here was comfort, if only we could get down.

Where did the French planes land? There were no harbors near the base. Did they land in open ocean? But those rollers? Though, of course, it was not always like that. The wind, today, had kicked up a terrific sea, even here on the lee side of the island. On a calm day, probably, they could land without difficulty in the partial protection of one of those big scallop-like harbors.

That, I supposed, was what we were trying to

do now, climbing up over the promontory, making a great circle over the hangar, around the radio towers and down over the sea, skimming over its uneven surface, then up the coast, looking for a calm enough stretch of water in which to land.

Round and round. The lift as we climbed over the promontory, the bump as we crossed the gully, the drop as we came down to the sea, turned and headed into the wind. Then that long "power drag," just off the water, suspended, almost touching the giant swells. Like a long sustained breath, that sweep up the coast, trying each harbor in turn, flirting with each; *You, I will choose—in a moment—in a moment—in a moment— You—but not yet—not yet—not yet—not yet— No.* Then the roar of the engine climbing again over the land, dropping again over the sea—holding off—holding off—holding off—

Lord—what big rollers, I thought, as we skimmed over the crests. It looked worse than Madeira and we couldn't land there—had to go on to Las Palmas. Would we have to go back today—to Africa? No shelter of course at Madeira, if we did get down. But here, once we got down, it would be all right. The harbor, the crane, the hangar. If only we could get down—then it would be all right.

This time, perhaps. Almost—almost—almost,

the plane sank nearer each second to the crests
of the waves. No—the long-drawn breath of the
engine poured itself out again in a roar of power.
Up over the promontory soared the plane, climbing into the air, its own element. A king, a god,
on top of all, it asked no favors here—not here—
not until it was once more down on the sea.

This time we would land, I thought, holding
my breath as we hovered. Yes, we had touched.
No, we were in the air. Crash. Yes, we had hit
the wave. Back into the air. What a bounce! A
blast from the engine. I waited for the second
spank. Crash again. Spank—spank—spank—spank
—would it never stop! Yes, we were down. We
had landed. But what a landing—had it ripped
the pontoons? But we were down—and now—

We turned to look at the harbor. It was behind
us, for we had landed slightly up coast. The
changing world of a few seconds before was fixed
for the time being. We did not see dozens of
bays passing below us. We did not see gully and
promontory and sea, all following each other in
quick succession in our view. No, we were here,
pinned to earth. We were fixed in this particular
bay. It was insignificant a few minutes ago, one
of many bays which we might choose to light in,
in a world of bays, rocks, hills, gullies, and waves.
Now they had all disappeared. Only this one remained, all important. This was our world now,

this bay, with its beach and its breakers, its great cliff on the promontory guarding the entrance to the harbor. We were dependent on it, tethered to it. Here we must stay.

It was true that we were moving, but our motion had not the freedom of motion in the air. It was part of a fixed pattern that revolved about us in unchanging repetition. The engine idled monotonously always at the same tempo. The wind roared past our ears always in the same direction. The waves broke into foam, receded, and broke again on the rocks. The plane rose and fell in even rhythm on the great rollers, and slowly drifted backwards down the coast.

A blast of the engine. We turned and faced the harbor. The rhythm broke. The plane rocked violently, headed across the waves, first one wing down and then the other, almost touching the crests on either side. Floundering clumsily, it struggled for headway. And the wind—the wind was now "side," blowing across the opening; turning us toward the shore, for our rudder no longer had control against it; forcing us, if we persisted in heading across its path, into the rocky headland at the mouth of the harbor.

No use. Couldn't make it this time, I realized. We turned, headed up the coast. Had to go back, drift down, and try again.

I glanced at our shelter as we went by. There

were only one or two houses and a few huts—but that hangar, and the concrete pier, and the radio towers!

And now there was a small rowboat coming out, pulled by two Negroes. There was another man standing up directing them—a white man, in a sun helmet. He waved a megaphone and shouted. We heard nothing—the wind, of course, sheathing our ears with a rushing sound. Never mind, we waved and made signals with our arms. Yes—we wanted to come in to the harbor. Could they help? A tow—a rope—?

My husband climbed down onto the pontoons and fastened the towing harness to the struts. I pointed the plane into the wind. The boat rowed nearer. They threw a rope. It missed, drifting down-wind from us. Again—there!—we had it. They started to pull, bucking the wind. Spray from the oars flew back in our faces. The boat made no progress. It was stationary. We were all caught in the rocking chop of the waves at the narrow entrance to the harbor. Only we were no longer drifting down the coast. We were held sideways by that taut rope, by the little rowboat, by those Negroes bending back pulling against the oars.

Were we stationary? We did not seem to be making any progress, with the wind pointing the plane in one direction and the boat trying to pull it in another. I looked at the point beside us, trying to measure any slight movement. I watched a jagged rock advance against a white patch of foam. I looked at the other arm of the harbor. Gradually I could see it protruding farther out to sea. The promontory beyond disappeared slowly. We were moving.

Once inside the harbor it went better. The chop smoothed out easily. The plane no longer rocked from side to side but went forward evenly with each little tug of the oars, the water rippling up over the sides of the pontoons. The spray on the rocks was behind us. It was suddenly very hot and still. Only the wind blowing down over the point, beat against our ears, hollow and distant like the roaring in a sea shell. We threw out our little anchor. The rope slapped down after it in curves and was swallowed up in the water. Enough—yes—it was caught now—on the bottom. The slack rope floated in coils on the surface. We were anchored.

CHAPTER III

A TRANSATLANTIC BASE

THE rowboat edged nearer, coming down-wind towards us, the two Negro boys dipping their oars lightly in the water. Their faces were beady and shining from perspiration, and their ragged shirts clung in wrinkles to their wet backs. They stared vacuously and good-naturedly at the plane, letting their oars trail bubbles in the rippled water.

The white man stood up, staggering slightly as he moved to the prow of the boat in an effort to speak to us. His face, pale and fleshy under the green-shaded sun helmet, was also perspiring. He had on an old brown sweater, full of holes and badly stained under the arms. His baggy trousers were held up by a belt drawn too tightly around a fat stomach.

"Monsieur," he said, smiling wanly. French, of course. I must translate. Was the plane all right here? "Bien amarré?" Did we wish to disembark? If so, our bags? The boys would take them. (The boys continued to stare up at the plane and smile good-naturedly, moving the oars slightly in the water. The line of bubbles changed, drifting towards us.)

No, we answered. The harbor was too small to leave the plane moored with a single anchor. If the wind changed, the plane would drift onto the rocks. It would have to be tied in three directions and held fast in one spot.

"Eh bien"—he would see if there was another anchor. "Madame," addressing me again, "pardon—you will excuse my appearance—I have a high fever—I am just now out of bed."

I looked at his drawn face under the shadow of the helmet. He was pale beneath his tan. There were flabby wrinkles below his eyes. Yes, he looked quite ill. "I am so sorry," I said, rather shocked. "Do you think you should be up?"

He made a grimace. "Mais non, Madame, I have a high fever—just now out of bed. But it makes no difference—no matter—I shall go back to bed when I finish."

Fever, of course—the African coast, yellow fever, malaria country. I wondered what kind of fever he had. Better not ask—wait until we got on shore.

A large and rusty anchor was brought out. Yes, that would do. We anchored the plane twice and tied it to some rocks on shore. Then, held from three directions, it was safe no matter what the wind did. Yes, now we were ready to go ashore.

No, we would leave our bundles for the time being. We closed the hatches and climbed down onto the pontoons. The shiny surface of the red wing was already hot from the burning sun. The boat creaked slightly as we stepped in and, headed into the wind, started for shore.

Before us the concrete pier blazed unbearably white and hot in the sun. It threw a shadow over the little beach toward which we were pointed. In this shadow two figures were standing, a tall man and a girl. I put my hand up to shade my face and eyes and looked at them. They were both young and both in sun helmets. The man was a Negro. No—perhaps not. He had finely chiseled features, not broad and thick like the two boys. But he was very dark, with almost a blue tinge to his skin. And he was so thin and long that his nicely cut and brushed dark suit hung on him listlessly as though on a rack, and showed no trace of the figure beneath. Why, he might be just poles underneath, I thought, like a scarecrow.

The girl was thin also, and wore a clumsy sun helmet on her head which looked as though it might extinguish her like the snuffer of a candle. It was probably a man's sun helmet, too heavy for that sweet sallow little face, for that flimsy cotton print dress flapping listlessly in the wind against bare brown legs, for those narrow feet showing dusty through the openwork sandals.

They came forward as the boat scraped bottom on the pebbly beach.

"Monsieur Leendbairgh—wel-come—" (Ah, he spoke English.) "I am here chef for the Company —here ees my wife—" She smiled rather shyly under the great helmet. She was very pretty with black curly hair and wistful dark eyes—a mulatto, perhaps, I thought. "Eef we can do anything for you . . . I have les telegraphies from France— Plees—" He bowed slightly and his thin hand, pointing to the open cave of the hangar, seemed to say that everything was at our disposal.

"Why—thank you very much," started my husband, "we would like to stay here for the night, if we could. Your mechanic has already helped us—" He looked around quickly, but the Frenchman had disappeared. He had taken shelter from the sun in the shade of the hangar. The fever, I remembered.

"We're well anchored here for the present," continued my husband, "but this harbor is open to the sea. Are there storms here this time of year?" The dark man leaned forward, eager and perplexed. My husband started again, "Where do you put the French planes? Do you hoist them up with the derrick and keep them in the hangar?"

The "Chef" bent toward us an expression of intense eagerness combined with pained confusion, as though he were trying to hear a very small sound at a great distance. He lifted up his hand to cover a nervous cough.

"You speek French? Je ne comprends pas, Madame?" He turned his narrow eager face to me.

"My husband says," I started laboriously to translate, "would it be possible to lift the plane out of the water into the hangar?" We pointed to the large black crane leaning over our heads.

"Mais oui, certainement, Madame." We moved slowly up the beach.

"Ask him," said my husband, "if they have any shackles to fit this plane."

"But I can't say 'shackles' in French—I haven't any idea—Monsieur, avez-vous des choses . . ."

"Comment?" He looked confused.

We made signs with our hands and pointed to the plane. We lifted an imaginary plane out of the water onto the landing by means of imaginary shackles. "Vous comprenez, Monsieur?"

"Ah—les manilles." (He understood and smiled. He was very anxious to help.) "We will look—in the hangar." He pointed again to the big shed above us. We started up the beach, our feet slipping back as we crunched through the loose stones.

The cement apron, running from the hangar doors to the pier, was baked hot by the unrelieved sun. Its smooth white surface was somewhat roughened by a reddish sand and small stones which had seeped over it in the wind. The crane itself, with its long arm and triangular beams, was mounted on a block of concrete which stood above the rest of the pier, the large hook swinging free out over the water. A rope dangled idly over the side of the block, and in the cracks of the concrete small weeds were growing.

I put up my arm to shield off the sun and push back the hair blowing in my face and eyes. The top of my head was hot to touch. We hurried into the shade of the wide open hangar. Out of the wind at last. The sudden stillness seemed more than a cessation of the wind. It was a positive quiet, like the positive coolness of green shade under a tropical sun, a still pool out of the rushing stream. We took a deep breath and looked around us.

On first sight the building had the familiar air of any big hangar at home. The same crisscrossing of steel rafters above our heads; the same ribbed look of the long walls, punctuated evenly with iron girders—all symbols to me of the competence and facilities of a modern aviation base.

And yet, it was strangely different. There was something lacking. Why all these modern facilities? Why the equipment and machinery? What purpose did they serve? For there were no planes on the concrete floor; no mechanics on ladders, tinkering with engines. There was no whirring noise of a busy machine shop; there were no engines on work benches, no propellers on the walls.

Shorn of all activity, the building looked, in spite of its modern construction, like a great empty barn.

In one corner, resting on a wooden carriage, sat an old speed boat, probably once used to meet the incoming plane. In the back of the building, half covered with a canvas, was a small tractor. There were coils of rusting cable and chains on the floor. Also, some discarded oil cans and a few empty barrels.

The Frenchman was leaning against one of the barrels when we entered. He came forward, put his hands on his hips, and stared at us questioningly.

"Monsieur—we are looking for—" I started again in French. We made gestures.

The Frenchman lifted his eyebrows, pursed his lips doubtfully. Well, he would look—

He went to the back of the hangar. He lifted up the rusting chains and let them fall again with a succession of dull metallic clinks. He went out of a back door. He came in again. He went out. We waited in the shade, listening to the wind outside, gentle, persistent, continuous, like a distant line of breakers. We waited, watching the bits of grit and sand chase themselves endlessly across the concrete apron. We stood, turning our eyes from the glare of the pier, the water beyond, the shining surfaces of the plane bobbing in the sun, back to the bare recesses of the hangar; to the tractor, motionless in the shadowed corner, the speed boat, put away on its rack, the chains, the barrels—all waiting, waiting. The girl scuffed a stone along the concrete floor, across the shadow to the sharp angle of sunshine which cut inside the hangar doors. Catching our glance, she smiled wryly and sympathetically.

Ah—he was coming, puffing from his exertion. He had some shackles. No, they were too small. They would not do; they would never hold the weight of the plane. He had no others? There was nothing else? He shrugged his shoulders and looked searchingly around the bare walls. "Il n'y en a pas," he said, discouraged, still staring at the empty walls, "perhaps in town . . ."

We turned to the tall "Chef." "Certainement, Madame, we will get some in Praia. There is a machine shop—we can send for some . . ."

He stopped speaking suddenly at a muffled word from his wife. Her impassive little face had lightened. She was listening to something. We all stopped talking. But it was only the wind, I thought, still persisting like a line of breakers, the sound of hundreds of little stones being thrown up on a beach. No, there was something else—a deeper, harder strand of noise in that long sigh, the sound of a car climbing uphill. We walked out of the hangar and looked up the slope, following the rough dusty road which straggled past three or four small plaster huts and rounded a corner out of sight. A few chickens scrambled in and out of the huts. Some Negro women were trudging up the road—but no car. Over the top of the tiled roofs, though, there was a small cloud of dust.

"See—a car!"

Soon it appeared, bumping around the corner, scattering the chickens to left and right and pulling curls of dust behind. It stopped with a harsh skid at the bottom of the hill on the sandy pier. The cloud of dust blew on past us in the wind. We ducked to avoid it and covered our faces with our hands.

When we looked up again, we could see that the car, under its coating of dust, was shiny and well kept. There was an official emblem on the radiator, and a chauffeur at the wheel. A Portuguese official stepped out of the back seat and brushed the dust off his uniform. He was sent from Praia by the Governor. He came up to us, clicked his heels and bowed. He shook hands, with my husband, with me, with the "Chef" and his wife. The mechanic had disappeared again. I wondered if he had gone to bed.

The officer started speaking first to the "Chef," in Portuguese. We stood and shifted our feet in the dust. The "Chef" turned to me, he coughed apologetically. "Madame, the officer says," he translated in French, "the Governor sends his respects—"

I turned to my husband and repeated again parrot-like, "The Governor sends his respects. He hopes you will come to Praia. He offers you all hospitality. He wants to know if there is anything he can do for you. Also they want to know about your papers, your passports—your clearances."

"Thank him very much," said my husband, smiling, "tell him we would like very much to see the Governor. We will call on him whenever it is convenient for him—also we would like to get some shackles—perhaps we could go right now, in the car?"

It was all translated into French and then into Portuguese. ". . . some shackles to lift the plane out of the water."

"Ah, of course, but you will come right away, with me—in the car?" The little officer pointed to the back seat of the open car. Yes, we could go. The "Chef" would go, too, and translate for us.

My husband looked back a moment at the un-protected harbor, at the shiny wings of the plane bobbing up and down lightly on the water. "It's all right with this wind—but if a storm comes up—" He looked at the sky. "Ask him," he said, "if they ever get storms from the sea."

"Monsieur, on n'attend pas des orages de cette direction là?" I pointed to the sea.

"Wind from the sea?" The "Chef" looked in the direction I was pointing, incredulous. "Jamais!" he said with emphasis. "Never—never—"

CHAPTER IV

"WE ARE LOOKING

FOR SOME SHACKLES"

WE climbed into the back seat and started up the steep hill, bumping over ruts and sliding stones. On the crest of the hill were two or three low huts, made of plaster and rough red volcanic rock. They faced the harbor, their backs to the wind, with small stone-enclosed yards in front, made again of loose volcanic rock piled up into a rough wall. Some Negro women pushed their heads out of the shuttered windows to watch us pass.

A great lurch over a worn dusty bank and we were on top. I turned to look back at the harbor but the dust, thick behind us, hid it from view. Ahead, one could see nothing but bare rough slopes covered with loose rocks and dry grass and a kind of climbing thorn. Was it burnt that strange browny red by the sun, I wondered. Or was it only the dust from the road that had covered everything?

I put both hands up to keep my hair from

whipping in my eyes. It couldn't be very far to Praia. When we were in the air this morning (Could it be only this morning? I felt as if several days had passed since then.) the two harbors had seemed right next to each other.

"How far is it, Monsieur, to Porto Praia?" I decided to ask the "Chef" at my left.

"To Praia—by car? Oh, only about half an hour —but it is a long walk."

Yes, it must be a very long and hot walk, I thought, over those bare volcanic hills, over that burnt thorny grass. But there were people walking it. Barefooted Negroes, in rags of European clothes, carrying great baskets on their heads, turned aside from the dust as we passed.

We sat back and prepared ourselves for a long and bumpy drive.

"Ask him," said my husband, "what time of year the Company operates from here?"

I turned again to the "Chef."

"From here?" he echoed, "the Company has stopped operating from here."

"Oh—" we said, waiting for explanations.

"The Chef has left."

"Oh—"

"Yes, I am now in charge. Before—I was radio officer—now, I am in charge."

"Oh."

So they were not operating from the air-base

and the chief had left. I wondered why. We sat in silence and looked out at the road. We were bumping down into a ravine. Here there were gray scraggly trees, their tops all bent in one direction, like seaweed swept along in the current. But the trees would never bend back again. They were caught, held in that tortured shape forever. The wind, of course.

"Madame"—the "Chef" turned to me—"will you stay in Praia—or near the plane with us?"

"Oh, we will stay with the plane, we always stay near the plane." Besides, I thought, that little harbor open to the sea—suppose the wind got stronger, or a storm came up, we would never feel safe about leaving the plane there. "We will stay with the plane, of course."

"Ah," said the "Chef," turning towards us with half a bow, "then you will stay in *my* house—the first aviators I have had as guests since I was made chef."

He coughed behind his thin dark hand and looked quite pleased. We all smiled and looked out at the road again. There were a few goats nibbling at the thorny grass, picking their way up the rocky slopes—the only sign of life except for the occasional huts with their sagging roofs and dirt floors. I wondered about the "Chef's" house. Would it be safe? Did the Frenchman sleep there? How about the fever?

"Monsieur," I decided to ask him, "how about the mechanic—he says he has a fever?"

"Oh, yes, he has fever," said the "Chef" wearily, spreading out his hands in a gesture of futility, "but it is just the fever we all get here."

"Oh—" We looked in silence at each other, at the white fingernails of the "Chef," at the back of the Portuguese officer in the front seat, at the bare volcanic hills, at the dusty road.

We sat in silence the rest of the way into Praia, until we started rocking down a hill into the valley. There were trees here, bordering the road, and we passed more huts sprawling with native children. The "Chef" lifted up his sun helmet, smoothed back his long black hair and replaced his helmet. "We are now," he said, turning to us, "entering Praia."

The women and swollen-bellied little boys ran out to look at us. Poor and dirty, the children wore almost nothing, their black skins glistening in the heat. Nearly every woman had on a red bandanna, a ragged calico skirt and shirtwaist, and, wound about hips and abdomen, a wide band of material making a heavy belt. It seemed to me a strange place for a belt, until I realized that the band was in exactly the right position to support the weight of a child if the woman were pregnant. And most of them were.

We climbed up another hill and entered the

town itself, which sat on a plateau overlooking
the harbor. We seemed to be out of the wind
here. There were trees and neatly painted houses,
pink and yellow. We drove along a narrow cob-
blestoned street which opened into a green square
of trees. We pulled up to a stop in front of a long
stone building. It was still, at last. No bumps, no
rattles, no wind, only the leaves rustling above
our heads and a few cocks crowing in the next
street.

"The Governor's House, Madame." Oh, yes,
we must get out. My hair was tangled and gritty
and my trousers covered with the fine red dust.

We climbed out. Up carpeted stairs into a large
empty ballroom with gilt chairs and one sofa.
The Portuguese governor came in. He bowed and
shook hands. His wife and daughter came in.
They were pretty and cool in thin clothes and lipstick. I wondered if the red dust from my trousers
would come off on the brocade sofa.

The Governor spoke perfect French. "Will you
not stay here with me in Praia?" he asked.

It was cool and quiet. I looked at the shaded
verandas outside the open windows.

"Thank you, Monsieur, but we must stay near
the plane."

"Ah, well, I understand, sit down." (We sat
down cautiously on the brocade sofa.) "What can
I do to help you?"

A servant brought in some champagne on a silver tray.

"You are very kind," I translated stiffly for my husband, "the car has already been of the greatest assistance. We are looking for some shackles . . ."

"Shackles?"

"Yes, some shackles to lift the plane out of the water into the hangar."

"Ah, yes, the chauffeur will take you to the store—"

We thanked him and shook hands again. Down the carpeted stairs; out into the hot street; off to the store. The "Chef" climbed out and bent under an open door, hung with pots and pans and strings of large square cakes of pink soap tied up in fish nets.

He came back, coughed into a handkerchief and started explaining, "No, he has no shackles, but he is sending a boy for some."

I translated.

"Can't we go there ourselves?" My husband leaned forward in the car and peered down the street.

We started off again on a narrow road, down a steep hill toward the harbor. The car bumped and lurched over stones. Little Negro boys leaned out of shuttered windows and shouted as we passed.

We stopped at the harbor master's. It was very quiet and the blinds were closed. "No, he is not here—but wait, perhaps—" A small boy scurried down an alley. A shutter flapped. We walked up the street. "No, he is back there." We turned. "Ah, he is here." A mulatto stood in a door, peering at us curiously.

"No, he has none," translated the "Chef," "but the mechanic says he can make some in an hour —*one* hour"—he held up one long bony finger to plead with us—"une heure seulement."

"That will be too late," said my husband, shaking his head. (Twilight in the tropics is not the same as in the north.) He looked out at the long shadow of the building across the street. The sun was already going down the sky. Unless we could get back before dark—

"Have they any cable—steel cable?" he asked.

"Un câble d'acier, Monsieur?"

"Un câble d'acier—perhaps—"

They all began talking together in Portuguese.

"Perhaps, yes—we will go to the machine shop. It is not far—"

We barged up the steep hill again, lurching around the narrow corners, up into the town itself. We stopped in a hot street, went through a door in a pink wall, through a dusty court into a machine shop—a garage-like room strewn with parts of automobile engines, bicycle wheels, uncoiled springs, chains, scrap iron, and horseshoes. We stepped carefully across the debris. There was no cable.

"No cable?" A man stopped hammering in the corner. Another Negro came up to the "Chef." He had some wire in his hands and they began to talk in Portuguese.

"No, no cable, but he has sent the boy for some." Footsteps scuffled out of the back of the shop.

"Can't we go there ourselves?" My husband looked at his watch. "It is—"

"But no, Monsieur, he is coming—just now— coming—"

We waited. The man in the back of the shop went on hammering. We looked at the anvil, at the piece of iron he was shaping. We looked at the walls, at a scythe, at an uncoiled spring, at a bicycle wheel. I began to count the spokes like a daisy. Yes—no, yes, no, yes—he would have some cable.

There was a window in the back of the shop, through which I could look. We must be very high, I thought, for I could see way down a valley, over those bare brown hills, glowing with a strange red light. Was it the late afternoon sun, or were they always that strange color, volcanic, as though lit by underground fires?

But beyond the hills was a green valley. There

were palms blowing in the wind and lines of
growing crops, sugar cane, perhaps, and coffee.
There must be lovely parts to this island, I
thought; cool valleys with the lush green of tropical forests; eucalyptus trees, with their long fingers rustling in the wind; bamboo, pushing up,
high and stiff and cool as sheets of water falling;
slopes covered with the dense dark green of coffee
bushes; gullies with streams running all year
round.

But not for us to rest in. For us there were
only these bare brown hills, those gray trees on
the slopes, bent in the wind, dusty roads back to
a harbor open to the sea, and waiting, waiting
until a boy came with some cable, "un câble
d'acier" so we could pull the plane out of the
water into the hangar. Yes—no, yes—no, yes—no;
he would not find the cable.

There was a sudden chattering outside in the
street. The man stopped pounding on the anvil.
"He is here." A Negro came in hurrying. He had
some cable.

My husband glanced at it. "It is too big."

The men all started to argue in Portuguese.

He fingered it thoughtfully. "But it can be unwound—it will do."

We hurried out to the car. A large crowd had
gathered in the hot street, men, women, and
children, their black faces shining with perspira-

tion. The women had limp babies, like wilting poppy buds, drooping on their backs. Some of them had baskets on their heads, balanced on red bandannas. They raised their hands and waved at us. The men shouted in broken English. We pushed our way through the hot, pressing bodies. Here was something waving that was not an arm. It was a claw, opening and shutting rhythmically, in the middle of those black hands. I stopped and stared at it, horrified, fascinated. It was a chicken's foot, torn off, held in the hand of a small boy who was manipulating it, pulling the tendons. He gave a delighted leer at my startled face.

We climbed into the car and started our long drive back to the harbor.

CHAPTER V

WHERE WOULD WE SLEEP?

IT was late afternoon by the time we bumped over the hill and saw the plane below us, still pointed taut into the wind. There were deep shadows under the opposite cliffs and it was cooler.

The mechanic was standing with arms akimbo just inside the hangar. We took out the cable. He shook his head disparagingly, as if to imply that he had known from the beginning it was hopeless. "No shackles, eh?"

"No, no shackles," we explained, "but this will do instead. It can be unwound."

He fingered it slowly. "Certainement, Monsieur, it will do. We can fix it, but it will take time—an hour or two, perhaps—"

My husband glanced quickly to the west. The sun was already going down behind the opposite hill. It would be dark before we could get started. He looked at the plane. It had not moved since we left. The anchors had not dragged. The wind was still blowing in the same direction.

"It's all right now," he said, "it's well anchored."

"C'est bien amarré—" echoed the mechanic.

"And if we can get someone to watch it tonight," my husband went on speculating, "in case a storm comes up— Ask him again," he said insistently, turning to me, "ask him if he thinks the weather may change before morning."

"Change?" queried the mechanic. "Mais non, Monsieur." He spread his hands out wide and let them drop again. "It never changes here—"

"All right, then, we'll leave it there for the night, we can take it up in the morning."

"Demain matin, demain matin—" echoed the Frenchman, nodding his head with evident relief as he went off.

My husband looked out at the waves beyond the point. "I think I'll row out and see what it looks like." He climbed into the rowboat and shook the oars into place. The two Negro boys picked up our bundles and looked questioningly at the "Chef's" wife.

At a nod from her we started up toward the old chief's bungalow. So we were not sleeping in their house after all, I thought, as we turned and faced the hill. I was carrying a cloth bag, full of papers and my radio log, and, slung over my shoulder, the camera.

We trudged up the rough road we had just

come down by car. The wind was blowing in our faces, blowing the hair back from my forehead, out of my eyes and mouth. But it did not seem like wind. It was something of more substance than thin air, more permanent and universal than a single scarf of breeze, rippling over a hill. It was more like a great river, a wave, which drowned the hill, and sheathed the island. And we, caught at the bottom of it, were struggling to swim against the current. It was a force that made every step more difficult and every load heavier. The camera weighed on my shoulder; my arms ached with the radio bag. And we did not seem to make any progress. Small gravelly stones slipped under our feet and slid downhill behind us.

We stopped halfway up the hill, panting. The boys set down the bundles. I looked back at the shadowed harbor, at my husband in the little rowboat. He was not yet past the plane. He was not halfway to the mouth of the harbor. I watched him bending and straightening, bending and straightening over the oars. How long everything took here!

We started up the hill again, passed by the little plaster huts, the stone yards, the chickens running in and out; and turned, following a footpath, along the side of the hill. I looked down again at the rowboat and the little figure in it, bending and straightening, bending and straightening. He was past the plane, but not nearly as far as the harbor mouth.

We stopped in front of a low bungalow, with a screen door bulging unevenly where someone had pushed it hurriedly going out. The boys put down the bundles and stared out to sea. The "Chef's" wife pulled back the screen door and fitted a rusty key into the inner frame one. It stuck and would not open. One of the boys put his shoulder to it. It swung back with a rush of air, lifting some papers off the floor of the dark room. We stepped inside. The screen door slammed.

There were newspapers on the bare floor, French ones, old and yellowing, gritty with dust, their emphatic black headlines staring up at the ceiling as they had been staring ever since the old chief left them there. And none of those things mattered now, I thought, none of those emphatic headlines, those photographed faces, those men hurrying to meetings. I wondered how much they ever mattered to Porto Praia.

The "Chef's" wife pulled up some cracked yellow blinds and opened a window. The blinds flapped idly, and some flies, wakened from their lethargy, drummed against the windowpanes. There was a large bed in the room, covered with a stained sheet. Against the wall stood a dingy painted bureau, propped up on three legs. The fine red sand had seeped in everywhere. The "Chef's" wife put her foot against the bureau to steady it and pulled out a drawer, looking for linen. I lifted up the mattress on the bed and looked under the hair bolster for bedbugs. But there were none—only dust. The "Chef's" wife pulled off the cover and threw the linen down on the bare ticking. She started to unfold the sheets. There were already dark, reddish marks on them from our dusty hands. She stopped and bit her lips with annoyance.

"It is so dirty," she sighed and looked at me wistfully. Would I mind? What would I think?

"Oh, no," I said. "It doesn't matter—I know we'll be all right here." We would be so tired we would sleep anywhere tonight, I thought.

But she hesitated and looked around the room anxiously, at the gritty papers on the floor, at the torn window-shades, at the marked sheets. She shook her head. "Tant de poussière," she said, picking up the sheets and folding them back into their creases. "It is too dirty—all too dirty— you must sleep with us, in our house. You can have our room; that is clean. Come—we will go—"

She looked out of the window, across the harbor to the long bungalow on the opposite hill.

"But this is perfectly all right," I argued. "We don't mind the dust—look at my clothes— Besides, we can't take your room. Why should we put you out? Really, this is all right."

She simply looked at me and shook her head. Perhaps she did not understand. The boys had already picked up the bundles. What should I do? What would my husband do? I looked out of the window at the growing dusk; the little boat was just at the harbor entrance, bobbing about in the chop. How long it took.

"Please," she said wistfully, "you will see—you will have supper with us anyway, and then we shall see the rooms."

"All right, then, after supper—" I agreed. I didn't want to hurt her feelings. We could argue about it after supper.

But how I wished it were "after supper" now; that I could lie down on that bed, without even taking my clothes off—lie down and stare up at the bare ceiling, like the newspapers, and let the door bang, and the shades flap, and the wind blow outside, and simply go to sleep.

We started along the thorny path downhill again. The stones rattled down inconsequently in front of us. We reached the bottom of the hill. The little boat was still bobbing about in the chop at the entrance of the harbor. We started climbing up the opposite hill. The wind was behind us now but it still seemed difficult walking. I stubbed my toe on a dusty ledge and nearly dropped the radio bag. My hair was blowing in my eyes and mouth but I could not brush it off as my arms were full. Every once in a while I would turn and face the wind, letting it blow my face clean. The little boat was out of sight, around the corner of the point.

We came to the top of the hill and faced the bungalow. It was long and narrow, with a low-roofed porch flanking both sides. Under the shade of the roof was a series of doors, a row of cubicles once occupied by officers of the Company. The doors were locked and the shutters closed. All empty. Only two rooms at the end of the building were being used by the "Chef" and his wife.

We climbed up the steps of the porch and opened the screen door into a small room. A large table filled the center of the floor. Against the wall stood a big cupboard on which were stacked plates, cups and saucers, cans of food, cracker tins, and several small bottles of medicine. A checked cloth hung kitty-corner over the table. In the center of the cloth was a small corrugated glass jar filled with toothpicks. A wicker armchair in the corner was softened by a faded, flattened out chintz pillow. The walls were bare. There were no curtains at the windows.

The "Chef" was sitting at the table, writing notes on sheets of lined paper. He jumped up as we came in, and swept his thin dark hand about the room in an explanatory manner, as though by that cordial gesture he might push back the restricting walls and open up vast resources of hospitality.

"You must not mind," he said hurriedly, "this poor house"—he coughed apologetically—"we are in the country."

"But of course," I said, "of course—it's very good of you . . ."

"No," said the girl, shaking her head, "it's very poor but—" She ended her sentence with a derogatory lift of her eyebrows, as if to say, "but what can we do about it?"

She led me through a swinging curtain into a second tiny room. There was nothing in the room except a large iron bed. A white coverlet hung down on either side to the bare floor. The coverlet was very white; and the iron bedstead, very black. There were no chairs. I sat down on the hard edge of the bed where the mattress, falling away from the sides, curved in towards the center.

"Here," said the girl, "you can sleep here—in our room." The Negro boys let the bundles down in the corner and shuffled out.

"Thank you," I said, "that's very kind of you but really, I don't think we ought to take your room. I'll talk to my husband—"

How long would it be before he came, I wondered. How long before we could have supper?

How long before we could go to bed? Was he still tossing about in the chop outside the harbor, or had he turned now, bucking the wind, coming back in the fast-falling dusk? I should like to sit right here on the edge of the bed, and not move until he came through the door.

CHAPTER VI

"I AM HERE CHEF"

WE were sitting in the little dining-room. It was almost dark. A warm patch of light glowed in the dusk just outside the open door. The Negro women were cooking supper in a small lean-to by the house. Their shadows now and then crossed the patch of light in front of the door, a flicker of movement in the stillness.

The "Chef" bent over his notes, sometimes drumming the tablecloth with his long fingernails. The girl, her arms crossed, sat motionless in the back of the room. She was so quiet that one forgot her presence. There was no sense of hurry, no stir of impatience in her attitude. She had simply drawn herself up into that knot of waiting, as taken-for-granted, as familiar to her as eating or sleeping. Her arms crossed, her feet twisted around the legs of the straight chair, she sat as though in a trance, her impassive little face staring out beyond her husband's stooped shoulders, beyond the open door, beyond the moving shadows, into the dark.

47

"Madame"—the "Chef" looked up from his work—"he is always out there—your husband?"

I leaned forward, creaking the wicker chair. "Looking at the sea—yes—l'état de la mer—"

"L'état de la mer"—he looked out of the door —"but it is always the same; the wind is no calmer—"

No, the wind was still blowing. Night had fallen; the sun no longer beat pitilessly on the white pier, on the hot roads. Twilight had come, and now this comforting dark, covering the plaster huts, the burnt grass, the plane pulling taut at its anchor. In the dark one could no longer see the clouds of dust, the bent trees, the slapping waves, the tugging ropes. But they were there just the same. The wind had not stopped. Under cover of darkness it was still blowing, stealthily, persistently, while people sat indoors, and ate and slept, forgetful. It was still blowing, still working, still sifting the sand over the concrete pier, in the cracks of windows, under doorsills; still swathing the arms of trees, still tugging at the ropes of anchors, as though goaded on by some resistless urge, on and on. Hurry, hurry, hurry, it seemed to say, as though there were not time enough to reach the places one must reach—not time enough to finish all the work one had to do.

Not time enough, I thought, half-humorously, looking around at the quiet room, at that girl, impassive in the corner with her arms crossed, at that man drumming on the table with his fingernails. Why hurry? There was all the time in the world. Time to waste; time to drum one's fingernails on the table; time to stare out at the wavering shadows; time to sit in a wicker chair and wait. Time didn't count here at all. It had stopped.

Listening to that wind roaring above us distantly, I had a sudden feeling of panic; a sense that it was life up there hurrying by, a great stream, tumbling, turning, sparkling, a rich swift life like the packed months just behind us. Labrador, Greenland, Iceland, Spain, the Azores, Africa; we were in that stream once, but now we had been tossed out of it. We here, on this island, were caught in an eddy, a backwater, out of the stream; a pool, where bits of sodden leaves and crooked twigs and stray maple seeds went round and round, and never made any progress, never won their way out again to the whirling current. A pool in time, where one climbed endlessly up shaley hills, and sat endlessly looking out of empty doors, and bent endlessly backwards and forwards over a bobbing boat.

Where could he be, my husband? He couldn't be looking at the sea now; it was too dark. I pulled myself out of the wicker chair and walked to the door. It was too dark to see over the hill. In the dimly lighted lean-to next door, I caught a glimpse of the Negro women cooking over a small stove. There was a delicious smell of something frying.

The "Chef" stacked his papers up on the cupboard shelf. "Madame, when your husband comes, we will eat." The girl got up and went to the cupboard for plates. She set them down on the table listlessly. Two for us, two for them, one more—I wondered if the mechanic would be there for supper. I looked fixedly at the fifth plate.

"There are only three of us here," the "Chef" said casually, following my glance, "my wife and I and my assistant, the other radio operator," nodding his head in the direction of the hill where the radio towers stood up in the dark wind. "No, you have not met him," he answered my questioning look, "he will come for supper."

I sat down again in the wicker chair. The "Chef" fingered the glass jar of toothpicks. "The mechanic doesn't count," he went on, "we cannot live together; we cannot get on—" He shrugged his shoulders a little sadly. "We were very good friends until the chef left—then, when I was made chef—" He spoke rather slowly and quietly, rubbing his nail down the side of the corrugated toothpick jar.

There was a silence broken only by the tinkle

of spoons in the girl's hand and the soft scuff of her sandals back and forth across the floor.

The "Chef" drew himself up in his chair and fastened the lower button of his coat. "I know that I am black"—he looked directly across the table at me, his long ascetic face drawn even longer in its taut seriousness—"but I can read—I can write—I can operate this radio station—"

"Of course," I said, "of course," nodding at him earnestly. He turned his head away from the table and coughed. His long fingers picked up the toothpick jar again and set it down. I looked at the girl. She was back in her seat at the end of the room, with her arms crossed. She had heard it all, quietly aware in the background. Many times before, she had heard it, and had accepted it patiently. There was nothing to do but cross one's arms and wait for something to happen. Once in a while something did happen.

Her face lighted up. She looked at me; and then made a little noise in her throat, that was hardly a word of recognition, to the "Chef." He pushed back his chair abruptly. Quick footsteps on the porch outside. My husband came in, stooping slightly, filling the door, the small room, looking about him, smiling apologetically.

The "Chef" stood up and straightened his coat. He looked erect, trim, self-assured. "Ah, Monsieur, it took a long time—will you eat now?"

The girl slipped quickly from her seat and came up to the table. Her dark eyes were alive, expectant, and wistful. I leaned forward on the edge of my chair.

My husband nodded good-naturedly and threw down his helmet. "Yes, yes," he said, and then, hesitating a moment, to me, "don't you want to go for a walk before supper?"

A walk? Heavens no, I thought, why should I want a walk; I had been walking up and down those hills all the afternoon.

My husband was looking at me intently. Oh, it wasn't a walk, I realized. It was something else; he wanted to talk to me.

"Pardon," I said as I got up, "un moment seulement—"

We went out into the wind and started walking downhill.

"What is it?"

"The mechanic," my husband explained hurriedly, "he says someone is very ill in that house, with consumption or something—I can't quite understand—you'll have to talk with him—he says . . ."

In the darkness below I could see a white shadow, a figure waiting for us, watching. It moved slowly towards us—the mechanic. He came up and nodded at me silently. My husband motioned to him and pulled my arm. "Come—let's

go this way." We turned and started to walk
downhill away from the houses.

"Monsieur"—I leaned forward to look at his
pale face, luminous and vague in the darkness—
"what is it? Someone is ill?"

"Oui, Madame," he muttered hurriedly, "it is
tuberculosis. The house is infected—c'est tout
contaminé—you must not stay there—" His voice
was tense.

"You must leave—" he insisted, "at once—and
use my house—or the old chief's on the hill
there." He waved his hand toward the gully.

"Thank you, Monsieur, thank you for telling
us—" (My mind went back to the bungalow, to
the "Chef" drumming his fingers on the table.
Such long thin fingers, almost blue under the
black skin—perhaps there was something to it.)
"Thank you, Monsieur, we will not use his bed,
of course, or the towels—"

The mechanic looked down at the ground; I
could not see his face.

We walked along in silence, the wind blowing
through my hair.

"Maybe we ought to see the other house," my
husband said at last.

"But he will be so hurt," I argued, "I don't
want to hurt his feelings—" I tried to explain in
French.

The mechanic looked up quickly. "You cannot

hurt his feelings, Madame," he said, dismissing the idea with a wave of his hand.

We walked along in silence.

"I think we'd better see that other house anyway," said my husband firmly. "We can decide about it afterwards."

The mechanic quickened his pace. "C'est un homme propre," he gesticulated eagerly, "always clean—it was always clean there. But over here—on this side"—he jerked his head towards the lights of the bungalow behind us—"tout est sale."

CHAPTER VII

THERE WERE OTHER ROOMS

IT was over half an hour later when we trudged back to the lighted bungalow for supper. All that time we had been climbing back and forth in the dark, uphill to get the key from the mechanic, down again, and up the opposite hill to see the old chief's house, down again and back up to our host's bungalow.

We felt embarrassed as we approached the lighted door, and stopped talking, as if we were spies entering the enemy's camp. Catching sight of their blurred figures through the lighted window, we had a sudden feeling of pity for them; for their unawareness of our eyes, and our thoughts. How should we break it to them that we were not going to sleep in their room? Not now—later. We would put it off until after supper.

When we came in they were all sitting around waiting quietly, patiently, as though used to waiting. They said nothing. The second radio operator, a pale mulatto, rose unobtrusively from the wicker chair and stood silently asking to be introduced. We shook hands and he sat down again. The girl took us through her bedroom to a little basin beyond, where we could wash. I poured the water gratefully over my hands and reached for a limp towel on a hook.

"No," breathed my husband tersely.

"What?"

"Don't use that towel," he whispered quickly, shooting a glance back into the other room.

"Oh," of course, I mustn't. ("C'est tout contaminé—tout est sale.")

I felt in my pocket for a small dirty handkerchief which I could use for a washcloth. Then, dripping wet, squeezing it out, I tried to dry my face and hands with it. They remained wet. I waved my hands about in the air. We went into supper, my hair still damp and sticky in the back of my neck and around my forehead and ears.

We joined the little group, my husband and I sitting side by side opposite the "Chef." The girl sat at the end of the table with her eye on the door. A Negro woman with a red bandanna on her head shuffled in and set down the food. There was cold meat, a dish of beans steeped in oil, and hard white rolls.

We were hungry and the food tasted good. The plates were clean, the table neat, but we were not at ease, not free to enjoy our supper or to talk spontaneously to our host. We were divided. It was as though we were only half there. Two people were there, sitting at the table, hungry, sympathetic, part of the group, inside the friendly circle. But there were two other people standing outside in the dark, looking in the lighted window—two outsiders, hostile, aloof, spying on that unconscious group around the table; watching the glasses to see if they were clean; watching the plates to see if they were washed; watching the napkins; watching the forks and spoons; whispering in the dark outside, "Tout est contaminé, tout est sale."

It was a silent meal. The smell of roasting coffee was pungent and delicious. The "Chef" coughed occasionally.

After supper, the second radio operator pushed back his chair, excused himself briefly and went out. The girl reached for a toothpick. The "Chef" got up and went to the cabinet for a bottle of medicine. He poured a pale liquid into a teaspoon and emptied it into his glass of water. He stirred it slowly. There was an intense silence, made of two people's thoughts converging at the same moment on the same point. I did not look at my husband. But we seemed to be breathing in unison. The girl picked listlessly at her teeth. The teaspoon tinkled lightly against the glass. Someone must speak.

"I have rheumatism," said the "Chef" casually, throwing back his head to take the glass at one gulp. "I must take medicine."

My husband shook his head sympathetically and evasively.

The girl looked at me. "You are tired? You will rest?" She made a little gesture toward the curtain behind her.

We *must* speak now. I looked at my husband. He shifted his chair and leaned forward. "Yes," he smiled, "we ought to turn in, but we don't need to take your room—"

"Comment?" The "Chef" tipped his chair abruptly and looked across the table at me.

"Mon mari dit," I started to explain, "we need not take your room, Monsieur, we can sleep in the old chief's house."

"Down there?" His eyebrows went up, startled, dismayed. "But no, it is dirty, it—"

"Oh, no, it isn't really dirty," we said lightly, "we have seen it—it's all right—"

"Ah non, it *ees* dirty!" He pushed back his chair and jumped up from the table. "The company has sent me word—" (His eyes were dark and intense.) "I am to do all I can for you. You will not use my bed . . ." His rising voice poised mid-air, the sentence unfinished, suspended, an impotent threat.

Then, lifting his hands in that familiar gesture of despair, he started again more quietly.

"Over there"—he shrugged his shoulders—"it is dirty—it has not been cleaned—"

He looked at his wife. She said nothing but her face went lifeless and empty. It had the blank look of snow on a dull day. Old snow on a hillside, unrelieved except for the wet dark trunks of trees. Her eyes were depthless like the unreflecting surface of those tree trunks. Her face was a pool into which one could drop a stone and there would be no ripple. She did not move but shook her head silently.

"Besides," he added wearily, "il y a des bêtes qui piquent."

(Bedbugs, I supposed.)

"Oh, well," said my husband cheerfully, "we have our own bedding. We always carry it with us in the plane. We can use—"

"Jamais!" exclaimed the "Chef" vigorously, "jamais, jamais." A long lock of dark hair fell over his forehead and he flicked it back impatiently. "With all the beds not being used in my house—ah, non—never—I cannot have you use your bedding—c'est honteux—here we have three, four rooms—" He pointed vaguely to the back of the bungalow.

Oh, there were other rooms—well, perhaps. We hesitated. We would see them.

We went outside and walked down the length of the dark porch. The "Chef" unlocked several doors and fumbled for a light. The building had electricity from the radio plant but there were no bulbs in the room. Finally he found one that would do. The naked bulb hanging from the ceiling blazed upon a bare room, cracked plaster walls smutted with cobwebs, an iron bed, a basin in the corner and an unpainted table. There were no chairs.

"Yes, this is fine—this will do perfectly." We tried to reassure them. The girl's face was unchanged. She went quietly for bedding. We got our baggage, our two bundles of clothes wrapped up in blankets, the camera and the radio bag, and set them down on the table. The concrete floor was gritty with dust.

The girl came back with the sheets and we started to make the bed. We shook out the bumpy hair mattress and slapped it into shape, pushing back the insides which were protruding in dark patches. The limp sheets fluttered from our hands and settled lightly in a wilted heap. They were thin cotton sheets, clean, but badly marked with large washed-out brown stains.

The girl gave a wry smile. "He used them for tablecloths—the man who was here."

"It doesn't matter," I said, "they are clean." We turned the sheet around and put the worst stains at the bottom of the bed.

Finally it was made, the pillow nicely patted,

the cotton cover tucked in smoothly. Only one stain showed, a lip of brown where the sheet turned over the coverlet. The girl stood back to look at it, and then at me.

She shook her head. "You have never slept in such a terrible bed," she said sadly. She spoke without emphasis. It was not an apology, nor a question. It was merely something set down in front of me, like those empty plates set down quietly on the table before supper. She started toward the door, not waiting for my answer.

"Oh, no, you don't know where I've slept—" I tried to say lightly. "This is fine—we are lucky to have a bed."

She was not comforted. "Il y a des petites bêtes," she repeated in the same tone, standing at the door, "les petites bêtes qui piquent."

They left us.

We started to unpack, untying the ropes around our blanket bundles. I sat down on the bed and looked at the stain. What difference did it make—we were so tired. Thank goodness, here was a bed we could sleep in, and the day was over.

Such a long day! When had it begun—how many years ago? I tried to think back into the past of this interminable day. Villa Cisneros—we were at Villa Cisneros last night, on the coast of Africa. Blazing desert; square Spanish fort; the Moors in their shadowy veils—how far away it seemed. We got up early in the morning (it was still dark), and we had gone to bed late the night before. A long Spanish dinner, starting at ten, going on until one. There was some very sweet strong coffee, and a woman had given me three ostrich feathers. And then we had gone to bed, dropping with weariness because we had come from— No, I couldn't think back so far.

How like a dream it all was, how unreal, and yet those instants had been just as real as this one. That room last night, crowded with cartons and painted furniture, had been just as real as this one. I had sat on a bed and wondered what I would do with the ostrich feathers. Now only this was real, sitting here on this bed, looking at the brown stain on the sheet, looking at the pillow, at the cracked walls beyond, at the dirty floor.

"Charles, is that a bedbug?" He looked down at a scrawly black beetle.

"No—too large—"

I started to undress. There was a black tick on the coverlet.

"Bedbug?" I stood up quickly.

"Looks like it." He picked it up between his thumb and finger.

"There's another on the pillow." We lifted it up and looked underneath. "And another, here."

He brushed one onto the floor and crushed it with his heel.

I moved away from the bed. "Look—there's one on the table."

"They're probably in the walls too." He looked suspiciously at the cracked plaster.

"Oh, let's go down and sleep on the plane."

"Well—wait a minute—maybe they're not bedbugs." He stepped on another. "We might try it anyhow—"

"I'm sure they are—she said—"

"I'll tell you what I'll do—I'll take one in to him and ask him if they bite—"

He went out quickly.

I stood in the middle of the floor waiting, conscious of every flicker of movement in the room, black beetles scuttling across the floor, pale nameless insects crawling out of the cracks in the walls, and those thin wispy bugs with long thread-like legs that dash themselves against the light. I shrank from touching the bed, the walls, the table. Here there was only one point of contact, with the floor, and if I walked up and down nothing could climb up my legs.

"Charles?"

He came in grinning broadly. "I asked him. He says, yes, they bite, but not badly."

"Not badly—!" I made a face. "Of course they *are* bedbugs—what'll we do?"

"Well"—my husband stopped a moment—"they may not like citronella—we might try that—"

"Oh, no, that'll be dreadful—I'd rather walk all night, or sit on the table—"

"You won't be safe from them there," he retorted. "You're all in—it'll be hot in the plane—we must get some sleep tonight—"

"Well—it's no use—I won't get *any* sleep in that bed. We don't know who's slept there before, either—do bedbugs carry disease? The mattress is full of those things—look at it—I can see five right now—"

"Where?"

"Two on the pillow—three—four on the sheet—five on the bedstead—there's another—six—seven—on the foot—"

"Eight—there's another coming out of the pillow—nine." We tore back the covers.

"Ten—down there in the crack—eleven." We pulled out the sheet at the bottom.

"Twelve—thirteen—fourteen on the mattress—Well—you win—" said my husband at last, "that's a little too much—we'll go. You stay here—I'll take the first load down."

We moved all the baggage out on the porch, clicked off the light and gently shut the door. I brushed and shook everything, the bundles, the boots, the mackinaws, the camera. Suppose they were already infested and we had to carry those dreadful things all the way across the Atlantic!

My husband picked up two bundles and went off around the corner. I stood alone on the porch, waiting in the dark. The wind was still blowing over the house, the rushing sound of a great stream. I walked out into the open, facing it gratefully, letting it blow back my hair, smooth my forehead, roar past my ears; letting it push against me, flattening the cotton shirt against my throat, my arms. It was cool, strong and fresh. It had come over hills, over the sea, from islands, from deserts, clean and broad as an ocean current. It would blow the bedbugs off. It would bathe me; it would wash me clean— Oh, lovely wind!

We walked down the hill together with the second load. I was not tired; I felt released. We had left that house, that room, that bed. We were free. Our plane was below us, sleek, shining, wind-swept, out in the harbor. Thank God, we didn't have to sleep in that room!

A three-quarter moon was coming up over the far hill. It showed dimly the soft outline of the hill, the hard outline of the hangar roof, against the sky. The square derrick-base loomed white and indistinct in its light. And there was a splurge of bright ripples on the water.

In the blurred shadow under the derrick was the darker shadow of the sleeping Negro boys.

Their crumpled bodies uncurled slowly as we approached. They got up and stumbled uncertainly down to the pebbly beach. There was no word spoken, no order given. We had come; they did not know why. We wanted to go to the plane, and unquestioningly they took us.

We pushed out over the waves in the little rowboat. No one spoke, the boys still heavy with sleep, the wind enveloping us all, like darkness. Into the silence of the night dropped the small sounds of our secret journey; the hollow knock of oarlocks, the creak of the boat, and the slow drip of oars gently clipping the water.

It was cool on the plane, the wind blowing strong and fresh. We repacked the bundles in our long baggage compartment, leveling them out, the hard ones on the bottom, the soft ones on top, to make a bed. Then we stretched out in our sleeping bag; the ribbed fuselage, a curved roof over us; the baggage compartment hatch, a little window to the sky. The plane rocked quietly and small waves slapped gently against the pontoons. We were suspended, I felt, swinging gently in a hammock in the wind. For, lying there quietly in the dark, we were acutely conscious of the wind; a many-stranded stream of sound, a river that had its deep current and its small eddies. Sometimes I was conscious only of the near sounds, the small surface eddies, the tapping, the whistlings around the plane. And sometimes I heard nothing but that distant roaring, leagues up, in the sky.

Now, to me half-asleep, it was not a river, but a wave, sucking strength from the ebbing waters, drawing in small stones and sand, rising menacing and dark before me. And I, a small child caught in front of it, too near to run back over the slipping sand, too far away to dive boldly under the green curl—I stood, watching it tower, watching it gather strength each second, ready to break in pounding turbulence upon me. A wave that climbed and climbed and trembled in its height —and never broke.

CHAPTER VIII

THE MORNING AND PLANS

I WOKE the next morning to a vague sense of insecurity, a feeling of unrest. Was it a dream I was struggling with, a headache, or some other physical discomfort? I turned over with difficulty and lay there a moment quietly, trying to analyze that numb and all-pervading feeling of discomfort, trying to localize it like pain. Slowly the impression hardened and took form. The wind was still blowing. It had not stopped at all. All night long, no rest. And here was the glaring sunlight of the next morning. I felt an intense weariness as if I too had been awake all night, with no rest, waiting for the wind to stop, for the wave to break.

But that was not all; there was something else. I opened my eyes and looked at the rounded barrel-like roof above me and the intricate tangle of wires and pipes on the back of the instrument board. We slept in the plane, I remembered—that room—those people—what would they do when they found out? What would we say to them? We should have got up early and gone back there.

Then it wouldn't have been so bad. Now—the best thing to do was to dress quickly and go up and explain.

We began to hurry into our clothes, knocking our elbows against the fuselage, the gas tanks; bumping our heads against the sharp backs of instruments. Some of the pipes were smudged with brown grease. We tried to wash from a canteen, with handkerchiefs. There was a good deal of sand on the blankets and our hands were beginning to be dry and sore. Our clothes were mussed and limp as we had used them, rolled up, for pillows. Hurry, hurry, we must get up there before they—

"It's no use—they're down here already."

Peeking through an opening in the fuselage, I could see the "Chef" and his wife. They were standing on the dock, watching the plane, waiting for us. Just like yesterday, I thought, looking at his lank figure under the sun helmet, at the frail fluttering cotton dress of the girl—only yesterday they were strangers. Today we were inextricably bound up in their lives. We knew how they lived, how they talked and thought, their likes and their dislikes, their weaknesses and their generosity. They had been kind to us and we had hurt their feelings. You could tell that from the way they were standing: he, erect, pole-like, lugubrious, his long coat carefully fastened around

him. He had an air of humble deference and at
the same time of formal dignity, like a distant
relative attending a funeral. She stood behind
him, a mute shadow, all his unexpressed feelings,
lying latent on her sallow pouting face.

Oh, Lord—what would we say to them? Better
not say anything. Simply let it pass as a matter of
course.

We rowed over casually and said good morning
with blank British cheerfulness. The "Chef"
walked down stiffly to the water's edge and held
the boat. I did not look at the girl. He drew himself up and coughed ostentatiously.

"You could—ah—not sleep—up there?" he said,
swallowing, dry-mouthed.

"Oh, yes"—my husband was casual and good-
natured—"we just decided to sleep in the plane,
we often do—it's very comfortable—"

There was no use going on. They were not listening. They were simply waiting for him to
finish what they knew he was going to say—an
excuse for the poverty, the dirt, the unkemptness
of that room. His words, robbed of all push of
sincerity, wilted like flags in a dropping wind.

We turned and walked up to the bungalow for
breakfast. The "Chef" and his wife had already
eaten. There were limp banana skins browning
on the used plates. The "Chef" waved us to the
empty seats. We sat down without saying any-

thing. One of the Negro women brought in a pot of coffee.

"This is very delicious coffee." I cast my remark out timidly into the quiet room; like a small stone falling in a still pool.

The "Chef" turned his long face toward me. He was frowning slightly. He shoved a dish of rolls across the table. "I am sorry," he said gravely, "that the bread is so hard, but it comes all the way from Praia. A boy brings it on foot—all the way—"

"Yes, yes, of course." (Hurriedly.)

We ate our fried eggs in silence.

Some men had come from Porto Praia to talk to us about our fuel. They were waiting for us at the hangar. Already all trace of the night's coolness had gone, burnt up quickly in the morning sun and the dry wind. Again the concrete apron was a blaze of white except for the partial shade thrown by the dusty car. Two men jumped out as we approached and brushed themselves off hastily. They shook hands and started talking in Portuguese, then more slowly in English.

"Colonel Lindbergh, we are glad to welcome you—we have your gasoline, your oil, ninety-five cans. It is all here—all ready. Here is the list."

The fuel agent handed the list to my husband and paused, beaming, waiting for approbation.

My husband smiled politely and took the list. (We'd never get off with a load like that, I thought, never in those rollers—never!) He looked at it as one looks at a letter which arrives after one has seen and talked to the sender. A letter which, had it come sooner, would have spoken with the conviction of flesh and blood; but now, cold and lifeless, it is only ink and paper, lacking all significance.

"You see," continued the agent, still beaming, "it is all there—it is all ready—" He shifted his stand a little, uncomfortably.

"Yes—yes," said my husband, "that's fine— fine—"

Everything was ready; the fuel, carefully planned for months ago, shipped, ready and waiting; the plane, shining and trim, bobbing on the water, equipped and packed. This whole place, I thought, looking around; the radio towers marking the top of the hill, the empty hangar, the concrete pier blazing in the sunshine, the suspended crane, and now the fuel—all ready. Everything ready, everything under control of man— except the wind.

"You will want it immediately, yes?" probed the agent briskly.

"No—no," my husband answered, "not right away—at least, not all of it—" He looked off for a moment at the whitecaps at the harbor entrance.

Then, turning back again abruptly, his voice hardened to precise fact.

"The wind never stops here?"

"Oh, yes," said the agent reassuringly, "oh, yes, it stops, but not now—not this time of year."

"When does it stop?"

"Well"—he paused to consider—"it will blow like this for six months—"

"Six months—and no calm?"

"No—never calm—not now—not for six months."

For six months that sound of a rising wave; for six months that long sigh! Did one get used to it finally, I wondered, or wait eternally for it to pause.

"But, Sir." The agent shifted his stand in the grit again. The heat was gradually climbing up from the concrete, thickening like some substance in which we were standing, now waist-high. "How much of your fuel do you want now? We can bring it this afternoon—this morning—if you wish—"

"Only about fifty gallons, at first, I think," said my husband, "then perhaps, we could let you know later—"

"With pleasure—with pleasure." The agent bowed, extended his hand. "We are very proud— we have had also the DO-X here—"

"The DO-X—when was that?" My husband's

voice hardened again into the stiff metal of conversation vitally important.

"Oh, some time ago, I do not remember—"

"Where did they land, do you know?" (Hard
metal.) He looked around at the group of people.

"They landed off there"—the "Chef" waved a
hand in the direction of the hill—"off the coast
behind there—"

"They were here some time," continued the
agent, "a month perhaps, or more—I cannot remember—" He turned to his silent companion
for corroboration. "I think they had some trouble,
some delay, I cannot recall now, something was
not quite right—conditions perhaps—" His voice
trailed off self-effacingly; then collecting himself
again, he swept his glance in a perfunctory fashion about the group, like a person about to leave
a room, making sure he has forgotten nothing—
hat, gloves, or cane?—no, nothing left.

"Well—good-by, Sir—your fuel will be here this
afternoon—good-by."

CHAPTER IX

"BRAZIL? HE TWIRLED A BUTTON"

"THAT isn't very encouraging," I said to my husband after they left.

"No—it isn't exactly—" He walked slowly down to the beach. "We'll see, though—I think I'll go out and look at the rollers again."

I started up the hill toward the old chief's house to wash and change my clothes. The "Chef's" wife had not suggested again that we use their rooms. Buckets of water to fill the cracked porcelain basins, and our rolls of clothing, had already gone ahead of me, carried uphill by the Negro boys. We were going to the Governor's for lunch. (The cool verandas, the brocade sofas, the women in summer dresses and lipstick.) How far removed I was from that world—I, in my dusty trousers climbing up this hill. Even if I changed my trousers for a cotton dress, unpacked a badly creased hat and some silk stockings; even if I spent the rest of the morning washing up with the water the Negro boys had carried up the hill— even so, washed, dressed, and combed, outwardly conforming to the code of civilization, could I ever really get back to that world? I felt we were separated from the Governor's house in Praia by a great gulf which could not be bridged by soap and water, clean clothes and a ride into town. We were separated by something else, of our own choosing, something I felt only dimly conscious of, yet I knew was there—some test of endurance, some ordeal by fire. Our contact at the luncheon table today (in our clean clothes, in our brushed shoes) would only be apparent, not real at all. Not real, like my contact now with the stones slipping away under my feet, with the thorns catching on my trouser-legs as I climbed; not real like my contact with the wind sheathing my ears as I pushed uphill against it, with the burning-glass concentrated on the top of my head, and with the thick heat I seemed to be wading through at each step. Nothing separated me from these things. They were mine, of my choosing and of my world. They were part of a pattern to be carried out, and as such they were real and acceptable. They were life itself.

I stopped, puffing a little from the exertion, where the path turned along the side of the hill to the bungalow. The wind, no longer blowing against me, unstopped my ears to the sound of its more distant roar, that great wave gathering strength. Down at the harbor entrance my husband was pulling at his oars again. Just like yesterday, I thought with a feeling of great weariness. And tomorrow would be just like today; and the day after just like the day before—on and on—I forever trudging up this dusty hill, he forever pulling at the harbor entrance—on and on—for six months perhaps, like the wind. I turned and went slowly toward the bungalow.

"Charles?"

The screen door slammed as he came in the house. The window-shades flapped in the room where I was washing.

"Well—" He came in slowly and stood in the middle of the room; he had reached a decision.

"Yes?"

"Well—I don't think we can get off here with a full load." He paused a moment and I looked up. He seemed quite relieved at the decision. "I'm going to radio Dakar and ask for permission to land there and reorganize."

"*Back*—go *back* to Dakar?" It seemed to me to be going down a hill we had just climbed up.

"It's only about four hundred miles. We can take off from here with a light load, and once we get to Dakar we'll be all set. Dakar's the next best place to start from. It's a French air-base, you know. No trouble getting fuel—good facilities, too—won't be any waiting there."

"Start off straight from Dakar—can we do that?"

"Oh, yes—been done lots of times. It's one of the nearest points to South America from the coast."

"It's two hundred miles further than here?" Hadn't we measured it on the map and found these islands nearer?

"About—but we can make it. We can throttle down and fly all night if necessary. There's a good moon."

"The moon, oh yes, of course, I'd forgotten the moon." I agreed hesitatingly.

He swept all my objections away, and with them some of the cobwebs of the place, all those myriad threads that seemed to be slowly fastening us down: the dust in one's hair, the sound of the wind, the heat, the rust on the machinery, the talk of fever, the tubercular cough. They need not, then, have dominion over us; they need not hold us down. They could be blown away. The forces against us could be tied up like the opposing winds of Odysseus and that one friendly force left out to sweep us home.

"I'll send the message off now—may get an answer tonight. And in the meantime," said my husband cheerfully as he swung out of the door, "we can ask the Governor if there are any other harbors around here."

I put on my mussed cotton dress and unfolded my creased linen hat. We took the long drive into town. I held my flapping hat with both hands. The dust blew in our eyes. We stopped under the shaded portico of the Governor's house. A man in uniform came out, and there were women in the background in summer dresses.

We walked into rooms, high-ceilinged and cool. I could wash my hands in the bathroom. There were purple hand-towels meekly folded on the rack, unopened and unwrinkled. There was a cake of unused scented soap by the basin, and a large bathtub. I was filled with a guilty greed, like a hungry person forced to be polite at a dinner party. If only I could make full use of this, I thought. By the laws of politeness I was only supposed to dabble my hands in the water. If only I could soak for an hour in the bathtub, tear the wrapping off the scented soap and muss up all the purple towels!

But lunch was ready. We went downstairs and sat at a long table. Across from me the Governor's wife and daughter glistened in white silk. We had a long and delicious meal. The Governor spoke beautiful French and talked to us about the Islands. They were discovered, we learned, probably by Cada Mosto, a Venetian explorer in the service of Henry the Navigator.

"Oh, yes, Henry the Navigator." (The familiar

name gave me a vague glow of pleasure. I could see his picture in the history books, a strange cap on his head and charts in his hand.)

"Discovered by accident, really," the Governor continued. "Cada Mosto was pushing down the coast of Africa but as he rounded Cape Blanco, he was blown out to sea by contrary winds—"

"By contrary winds?"

"Yes, you know our winds. He was blown onto the Cape Verde Islands—at least Boavista and Santiago he discovered. (*Do* have some more chicken, Mrs. Lindbergh?) There are two main groups, you know, the Barlavento (or Windward) Islands, and the Sotavento (or Leeward) Islands."

"And we are in the Leeward group?"

"Sotavento, yes. In the Barlavento group the trade wind blows steadily all year. Here, there is some variation—in the rainy season—"

(A fresh roll was laid down at my place.)

"When is the rainy season?" I asked.

"The rainy season is just over. It lasts from August to October. Now, we have started the dry season—of constant winds—from November to May. Then, of course," he added as an afterthought, "there is the harmattan—"

"What is the harmattan?" I asked, shocked as though introduced to a new member of a family I thought I knew well.

"The harmattan is our hot wind that blows

from December to February—very hot and dry.
It comes from the desert, you see, and carries
fine specks of dust and sand." (He pinched his
thumb and finger together to show the size.)
"Sometimes the Islands are covered for months
with a thick yellow haze—"

"But aren't your crops all burnt up then?" my
husband wanted to know.

"Oh, no, we have valleys watered by streams
all year round. We can grow a great many things
here, sugar cane and sisal, oranges and physic-
nuts, coffee—"

"This coffee?" I interrupted, holding up my
cup.

"Of course, this is our coffee. You like it?"
The Governor smiled. "I will give you some."
(We nodded politely.) "Only you must be sure
to make it properly. First, it must be roasted in a
shallow pan— Look, I will show you—"

He sent for some beans roasted to exactly the
right color.

I sat back in this easy, comfortable, and completely unreal world where there was no pressure,
no sense of time, no urgency. One could talk for
hours of the history of the Cape Verde Islands, or
discuss their produce. One had time to roast coffee
to exactly the right color, time to discuss anything
theoretically.

After lunch, the Governor sent for charts of

the Islands, and a table to spread them on. He uncurled them and weighted down the corners. We looked at the Islands, neatly contoured and marked, set in a flawless paper sea. Santiago, Santo Antão, São Vicente, Santa Luzia, São Nicolão, Sal, Boavista, Mayo, Fogo, Brava: surely among all those islands we could find a harbor to take off from. The Governor pointed out one or two. None of them were land-locked, but still, on the lee side of an island, one of those big scallops ought to give enough protection. They looked quite sheltered. But so, in fact, did Porto Praia. There were no lines on that neat black and white chart to show the rollers coming in. There were no streaks to show the wind.

It was not on a chart, I realized, that our problem could be worked out, but on water and land, in a harbor like the one we had just left, with the dust and the wind and the rollers. It could not be done with a ruler and pencil, but only by bending and straightening over a little rowboat in the harbor entrance, only by climbing up a dusty hill against the wind. We must go back.

"But you will not stay?" urged the Governor kindly. "You could stay here. You could be quite comfortable." (I thought of the purple towels, the scented soap, the delicious food.) "We could get more information for you—more maps—perhaps in one of the other islands you could find . . ."

They smiled sympathetically. I felt warmed by their kindness and understanding. But it was no use; the answers to our problems were not in the information they could give us. If only it were something else we wanted: facts about the early slave traffic from Africa, sisal or eucalyptus oil, baobab trees or coffee. It was like the verse of Emily Dickinson.

> Brazil? He twirled a button.
> Without a glance my way:
> But, Madam, is there nothing else
> That we can show today? [1]

No, nothing else—thank you.

"Thank you—thank you for the coffee, too—no —thank you—we must go back to the harbor."

[1] From *The Poems of Emily Dickinson,* Centenary Edition, edited by Martha Dickinson Bianchi and Alfred Leete Hampson. Reprinted by permission of Little, Brown & Company.

CHAPTER X

BACK TO DAKAR?

OUR fuel was waiting for us when we got back to the harbor. There it was, the familiar square tin cans piled in a block on the white pier, their shiny sides flashing in the early afternoon sun. They seemed strikingly incongruous on that sandy pier, against the empty hangar. They were so new, unwrapped, and fresh. They lent a kind of vigor to the place we had not seen there before, a sparkle of life.

Our friends at that station seemed to feel it, too, for they were all down on the pier gazing at the pile. The "Chef," erect in his loose gray coat, had just supervised the unloading. His wife, a little awed by all the bustle, stood watching in the shade of the hangar. Things did, then, actually happen here. People came, wanted fuel, wanted help, and her husband was managing it.

The mechanic was out, too, in his brown sweater and sun helmet. His sleeves were partly rolled up and he was ready to take charge of the refueling. Here at last was something to do. Here was something he understood better than anyone

else. He would show them—even in this out-of-
the-way spot—people knew their jobs.

Even the two Negro boys were out, sitting in
the rowboat, waiting for instructions.

They were pleased to see us arrive. Now things
could begin; now they could start.

"Monsieur—your gas—you wish to refuel now?
We are all ready—"

"Yes—yes—that's fine—might as well—but I don't
need it all now. [*To me.*] Tell them I only want
ten cans—only enough to get to Dakar."

The Negro boys started to load up the boat.
The mechanic went for a hammer and chisel to
open the cans. I stepped back to talk to the girl.

"Here," I said, "is some chocolate—un petit
cadeau—we thought you might like . . ."

She did not understand at first, peering with
a troubled look into my face. I had to explain
again, "C'est pour vous—for you," putting it into
her hand. She smiled very shyly. Then I showed
her the coffee from the Governor. "Perhaps we
could have some tonight. He said it should be
roasted . . ." Oh, yes, she understood; she would
roast some. Would I come up to the house with
her now and rest; I must be tired?

I was very tired—splitting headache—must be
the sun—but where would I rest in that house?
Not in their room, and not with the bedbugs. No,
I would lie down in the baggage compartment.

"Thank you, but I think I will stay here while they refuel. We will come up later, when you have tea."

She went off nodding, carrying the bag of coffee and the chocolate in her sun helmet, shaded under her arm.

Only enough to get to Dakar, I thought, stretching out in the baggage compartment, pushing my coat under my head for a pillow. That's decided, anyway.

That's a relief. No more waiting around here on the chance of finding a better harbor. (There weren't any, anyway. We could see that from the charts.) On the chance that, in a light wind, on the lee side, in the partial protection of one of these coves, one might perhaps—no, no more waiting on the chance.

It had looked like a good place to start from, too. After all, the French had picked it out for a transatlantic base. And we would have saved over two hundred miles. But now we knew it was impractical, it was better to go back to another harbor, a good port, with supplies, fuel facilities —everything, there. Back to Dakar.

Well—that was decided. They were putting in the gasoline now. I could hear the crimple of tin as the cans knocked against each other in the boat. Then the metallic thud as one of the cans was set up on end, and then—bang—bang—bang, sharp tinny blows on the top of the can. There, the chisel was through. That's one hole anyway. Now the other—bang—bang—the tin reverberated metallically to the indistinct confused murmur of voices.

Then the voices stopped—silence—nothing but that rushing sound. Was it the wind, or could I hear the gas streaming into the funnel? Yes, that's it. Here, a moment later, came the unmistakable fumes of gasoline drifting back to me. Hot and sickly sweet. I knew, I had watched it so many times, seen the escaping fumes curl over the wing like a transparent fire. The wind was blowing them, right back over the cockpits, pouring them into my compartment.

It would not make the headache any better. There, it was clearing a little—that's better—I could breathe. Bang—bang—bang—they were opening another can. Only enough to get to Dakar, anyway. Once the gasoline was in, we were all ready—except for the radiogram. Perhaps that would come this afternoon. Perhaps we could leave tomorrow morning. Bang—bang—

There was the gas again. Perhaps if I shut everything, the hatch, the door— No, it would still seep in through the cracks. And it would be even hotter. There wouldn't be much more anyway.

Bang—bang—bang—I wished they would open

all the cans at once, not jump those bangs at me periodically like that. I lay, waiting for them, and then they fell like the blows of a hammer, right on my head. Bang—bang—bang—he didn't get it the first time—there it goes.

I could get an aspirin and some water out of the canteen. But the canteen was in the bottom of the compartment, way under the bag I was lying on. We put the hard things on the bottom last night. It would mean moving everything, and such an effort, and such pounding in the temples. Yes—it must be the sun—everyone else wore helmets. Bang—bang—bang.

Besides, would it do any good anyway? Was it *me* that had the headache? I wasn't sure, lying there dully, looking up at the ribbed fuselage. Wasn't the headache out there, outside somewhere, in those bangs? Wasn't it in the wings of the plane, the hot shiny lacquer? Wasn't it in that dusty pier? Wasn't it in the burnt grass and in the wind? Not in me. "It" had the headache—the island, perhaps, or something that brooded over the island, and I was just caught in it, a little part of it, a single throb. Bang—bang—bang. They couldn't be much longer—only enough to get to Dakar.

CHAPTER XI

CONTACT

THE radio operator was to contact Dakar again at five-thirty. There might be a message for us. Would we come up to the station to get it? My husband stuck his head through the hatch to tell me. Of course, we would go up to the station. I scrambled out of the baggage compartment. We shut the hatches, dropped down into the rowboat and started off.

We climbed up the dusty hill, a little more cheerfully this time than ever before. Now all would be settled, all would be clear; we were going to Dakar. The radio towers, rising before us on the crest of the hill, seemed symbolic of our hopes. We pinned our faith to them, letting them draw us uphill, like the beam of a lighthouse pulling a sailor into port. Towering above our heads, erect and pencil-slim, they seemed unmoved by the wind, buffeting against our backs; untouched by the sun, still slanting in our eyes. Spanning with their tenuous wires the little radio house below; overlooking in their dizzying height the small bungalows and huts, the harbor, and even the

89

island—they seemed to reach up to another world, that Olympian world of power, speed, vision, which we once had. We would have it again. To-morrow morning, perhaps, we would be back in that world—now we were going to Dakar.

Once inside the radio house, we felt more cheer-ful, more ourselves, than we had anywhere on the island. It was not only the happiness of our errand; the whole place breathed an air of success, effi-ciency, and power. The big motors, their housings well dusted, their shafts well oiled, were serene behind neat cages. The radio sets with polished dials and panels, the extra earphones hanging on hooks, the neat desk with its empty baskets ready for messages, the calendars and lists of stations pinned up on the bare wall—all spoke of daily and efficient use.

We were enclosed here, too, out of the wind and the sun. There was only one small, rather high, window to the sky. Buttressed on all sides by these whirring machines, symbols of power and control, we felt completely cut off from the rest of the island, but not, oddly enough, cut off from the world. Why was that, I wondered. What was it that connected us? Not simply the miracle of com-munication at our command. Not merely the simi-larity between this room and other rooms out in the living world. (We might be anywhere—in a great city or on an ocean liner, in the north or in the south.) No, this *was* the living world. There was a live connection, an organic tie.

I turned around curiously to look at the other wall. There, staring down at me from the mouse-colored plaster, like a round eye, was the startling face of a clock. An ordinary blank-staring clock, the hands pointing meticulously to five-twenty-eight. So surprisingly familiar, so shockingly incongruous, I had to collect myself before realizing that this was, perhaps, the first clock we had seen on the island. The island *did* go by time, then, I considered with some effort—by black-and-white numeraled, steadily ticking, round-the-white-face-of-it time. At least, this station went by time.

Of course, we had gone by time. There were our chronometers to be wound every morning. But they did not seem to have any connection with the time of the island. They were arbitrary instruments we had brought with us from another world, shells from the floor of the sea, still faintly echoing the rhythm of another life. And when we took these time-pieces carefully out of their cases, like polished jewels, wound them, looked at their precise faces, and slid them back again, they were, in a way, quite meaningless, though precious, reminders of what was going on in the world outside. Like nostalgic exiles reading in old forwarded newspapers the weather at home on a date long past: "July 8th. Cloudy—light showers—clearing

toward evening—" so we would read with quaint
detachment, looking at those hands. "It is eight
o'clock in Greenwich." In Greenwich, yes, but
here—now? Where—when? It was hard to tell
what time there was on that island. One lived ac-
cording to the wind, hunger, sun, sleep, and
night. How long had we been there? Could it be
measured in weeks, days, or hours? I couldn't tell,
looking back wearily.

But now—and this was a "now" that I could
name, looking up at that bald round eye. (The
minute hand hopped unaccountably like an insect
to the next division.) Now, it was five-twenty-
nine. It was five-twenty-nine in that unseen station at Dakar. And it was some other equally precise time in Natal across the Atlantic, in Las
Palmas behind us, in Julianehaab on the tip of
Greenland, in Paris, in London, in New York.
Not the same time in all those places, but a time
that had a definitely understood and accepted re-
lation, second by second, to each of the other
times.

Was this, then, the cord that connected the
station to the rest of the world? The schedules,
the calendar, the time-tables, the clock? And did
this tenuous thread hold the entire world together,
place to place? A life-rope, propped up artificially
here and there, sinking under the water in other
places, allowing one to walk precariously in shift-

ing tides. It was all right as long as one hung on to the life-rope. But suppose one let go for a second —what then? What currents, what whirlpools, what undertow, would suck down the careless! One would be drowned, hurled, tossed, at the bottom of the sea. Astray forever in an alien world, where fronds of seaweed waved without a sound on bloodless bones of coral.

What a nightmare—what an abyss to look into —but no, we still had hold of the rope. There was that clock. The eye on the wall blinked again—it was five-thirty. Right on time. That quiet little man in the back of the room, pale, impassive, efficient—he had his hand on the rope, too. His head incased in earphones, his fingers on the dials, he looked at the clock, his window to the world.

He was not watching us. He was not aware of us; he had already reached those outer realms. Switches flashed off and on. The heavy whir of the dynamotor, the squeak of the key, and then silence. He was listening; he reached for a pencil. He had them, then, he had Dakar! At his fingertip he had Dakar. Living proof of that bond with the world. Touch of flesh and blood to the doubting. Sound, mind, spirit, cutting across space, over water, through wind—unwavering, undeterred, like light through darkness. But we also could cut across space, over water, through wind.

We also could touch Dakar, almost as quickly, almost as easily as that, with our plane. In a few
hours we could reach Dakar—at a word, at a
touch, tomorrow perhaps—

The message was coming in now, dribbling into
the earphones, dribbling down in words on the
radio form. We slipped behind the desk to watch
it. First, all those preliminary introductions neatly
put into cubbyholes on the paper: "Point of
origin: DAKAR—Date of origin—Time—Destination: LINDBERGH—CRKK, PORTO PRAIA—Number
of words in message." Then slowly, in the same
lifeless sleep-writing script, words—English words
—a message. I caught them over his shoulder, my
eye fastening on important ones: ". . . TELEGRAM
RECEIVED . . . BEG TO INFORM . . . IMMINENT
DANGER . . . YELLOW FEVER . . . QUARANTINE
. . . IF WE CAN BE OF ANY ASSISTANCE . . ."

The operator tore off the sheet deliberately and
put it in a tray. His impassive face had not
changed. Pale, expressionless, and efficient, he
turned back to the dials, fiddled with them a little,
adjusted his earphones, and went on tapping at
the keys.

Can't you *read?* I wanted to cry out—can't you
see what this means to us—how can you go on like
that?

My husband picked up the message and read it
again. He said nothing, his eyebrows raised, half-

humorously, half-quizzically. His face had a slightly twisted look as though he had unexpectedly tasted something sour.

I looked at the "Chef." His face had suddenly shot up in horror—like a candle-flame soaring to twice its height, trembling in its intensity and brightness. "Yellow fever!" he spurted, leaning across to my husband. His eyes were the only feature in his face at this moment, burning and dark with anxiety. "But you will not go?"

"Well," said my husband, a little wryly, "guess not—we'll see . . . Have to think about it—"

We turned to go out of the station. The eye on the wall blinked again maliciously. The key went on tapping mechanically in the back of the room. We drifted slowly past the inanimate machines, and walked out—into the wind.

CHAPTER XII

YELLOW FEVER

WE went back to the "Chef's" bungalow. I sat down in the large wicker chair in the back of the room. The girl came in with the teapot. Now, I thought, trying to rouse myself, I should make some effort. I should get up from this chair, out of the sunken cushion. But I did not get up; I continued to sink back heavily in a kind of stupor. My husband and the "Chef" were sitting listlessly at the table. The girl scanned our faces curiously.

"Yellow fever!" said the "Chef," jumping up with some animation, "yellow fever at Dakar," passing on his piece of news to the girl.

"Ah—" she said, her face pursing up into a grimace. One of those strange grimaces, so peculiarly Latin, that completely change a person's face, chilling you with a suddenly different aspect; and showing you, more clearly than any words, the pits of horror that were climbed through before such an expression was learned.

She set the tea things down on the table and we drew up our chairs.

"Yes—yellow fever—" continued the "Chef." "They cannot go—" He dropped two pieces of sugar into his tea.

My husband nodded absently.

"Mais non," persisted the "Chef," leaning across the table, "you cannot go—"

My husband said nothing, still nodding absently.

"But you know," continued the "Chef" doggedly, "yellow fever—it attacks the Whites much more than the Blacks."

"Does it?" I leaned forward in my chair, impressed by the intensity of his gaze.

"Ah, yes, the Whites—they last no time at all." The corners of his mouth went down in an expression of cynical abandonment. "On vomit de sang et—putt"—he snapped his fingers dryly—"c'est fini!"

"Oh—" I said, still staring at him. I did not think it was necessary to translate this for my husband. Every once in a while the "Chef" turned to his wife as if for corroboration. Her sallow face still held the faintest remembrance of a grimace, hidden in the corners of her mouth and the lift of her eyebrows. She watched him without saying anything.

"She had it," continued the "Chef," nodding at his wife, "and survived—but three sisters and a brother died at the same time."

The girl gave a ghost of a nod and went on stirring her tea.

She was white, then, I thought, looking at her pale face.

"She is Italian," explained the "Chef" quickly. "She was born on the Islands."

The girl, still stirring gently at her tea, did not look up.

"I also—" he said, coughing ostentatiously—"I also am part European, although I am black. But for us Blacks it is not so bad—the fever is not so bad. For you, though—" He coughed again and lifted his teacup.

My husband got up and went out. Now, I thought, I must get up from this wicker chair—but I did not get up.

After a while I went out and sat on the porch-steps with the girl. We did not speak to each other, both looking out over the knob of the hill to a horizonless sea. It was getting dark rather fast, the land already a blurred mass of shadow. Only the lifted-up faces of the waves still held that greenish after-sunset light, unearthly and cold like a submarine glow. The wind seemed quieter for some reason tonight, as though to reconcile us to our enforced stay on the island. It persisted still, a constant and even sigh; but it was more the sound of a ship pushing ahead through water, the great waves curling back on either side from the keel.

As the darkness fell abruptly over us, and only the lips of the waves below were luminous, I felt that we too were on a ship pushing out into an empty sea. Quite alone, only the girl and I on the prow, being carried ahead swiftly toward what I did not know. Only motion could create that perpetual breeze; only speed could cause that constant unrest. Now even the tips of the waves were blotted out in darkness. All bearings were lost, outside our huddled forms. And I had lost that fundamental fixed feeling of land. No longer rooted, I seemed to feel the sway and tip of a boat. How could I have gone so desolately far away from reality? I turned to look at the girl for reassurance. What did she feel, staring out with blank eyes into the blank darkness?

With a little sigh, she drew up her bare knees under her cotton skirt, and hugged them to her thin body.

After supper my husband and I started back to the plane, dead tired. There was no discussion about where we were going to sleep tonight. It was simply accepted. We walked in silence down the hill. We had not been alone together since we received the radiogram. But I did not ask what we were both thinking, "Well—*now* what are we going to do?" One learned, even as a child, that there were certain boxes (Japanese ones given for Christmas) that there was no use opening. There was nothing inside. So we did not say anything to each other about the radiogram, but quickly went to bed.

It was the same kind of a night as before, too hot inside the sleeping bag and too cool out of it. We slept badly. I had nightmares—all those bad dreams one had as a child when there were too many bedclothes. They tumbled one after another in confused succession all night long.

And then finally, toward morning, there was the escape dream. You are running; they run after you. But don't look behind. Into the empty house—but they pound at the door. Upstairs like a cat—but their feet on the steps below. Up to the attic—hidden at last—but their shouts in the hall. Quick, there is always the skylight. Did you forget you could fly? Crash with your head through the glass! Flap with your arms—hard, hard! Once you get off the ground it is simple—once you get clear. The first few hops are the hardest— But their hands on the knob. Oh, Lord—only get through the hole—up in the air—all of you, even your feet —too high for someone to reach and pull you down by the toes!

CHAPTER XIII

THE EMPTY BOX

THE day began again, this same day we had lived through so many times already. Looking ahead was like looking back at yesterday. Only today, there was nothing to wait for, no message from Dakar. We would have to make a decision, find a new way out.

"I think," said my husband deliberately, hoisting himself out of the cockpit, "I'll radio Bathurst and ask for permission to land there."

"Where is Bathurst?" I asked.

"British Gambia—on the coast—just below Dakar—"

"Is it further away than Dakar?"

"No, it's really a little closer, a few miles."

"Will it be just as good?" I was doubtful.

"Just about—it's not a transatlantic base, but it's a fair-sized settlement with a big harbor. We can make a night flight to South America, if we have to—with a moon. Let's see—" (He considered for a moment.) "Yes, we'll have a good moon if we start this week." (He dropped down onto the pontoon.) "I'll send the message now—we might get an answer tonight."

"Yes, I suppose we might," I said, not too hopefully. If there were yellow fever at Dakar, why wouldn't there be yellow fever at Bathurst, too, right next to it?

At least we had something to wait for. We had a peg on which to hang the shapeless hours: "We might get an answer tonight." But, in the meantime, the day stretched ahead like a long road. We already knew all of its landmarks; and only wished to pass by them as quickly as possible. It was an empty box, which we wanted to fill with anything, no matter how trivial, in order not to stare any longer at its emptiness.

There were always certain regular duties to be performed, part of the constant care needed to keep the plane in flying condition. After breakfast we started on this familiar routine, continuing doggedly all morning, stopping only for the long walk up the hill to the bungalow for lunch.

First, there were the pontoons to be pumped dry. A little water always seeped in even while we were at anchor and, unless taken out regularly, soon added many pounds to the weight of our plane. My husband got out the bilge pump. I unscrewed each pontoon cap and put it aside carefully where it would not be knocked off into the water. Then he would put the hose down into the bottom corner of each compartment. Kneeling on the end of one of the pontoons, I would hold it in place while he pumped until the last drop was sucked out, then he screwed the cap back again firmly.

Next, the fittings and wires which had been in the salt spray must be greased. My husband daubed on the heavy yellow grease wherever there was a trace of that fine white powder which marks the corrosion of aluminum. Then he wiped oil over the propeller blades where they had been splashed with spray on our landing. The polished metal was spotted with small white rings of salt. He squirted oil on the hinges of the ailerons, the rudder, and the elevator, to ward off the dull brown stain of rust that slowly attacks steel.

The surfaces of the plane, too, needed care. They were beginning to show the effect of the constant heat of the sun. The wings burned so hot you could hardly press your hand against them. The color, which once glowed a brilliant flame, waxed and shiny, was gradually fading to a dull orange. It had the flat burnt-out look of an old car, left out in the desert, beaten by sun and dry winds. The paint was beginning to show cracks, like lines of age, the first fine wrinkles in a woman's face.

What a constant battle it was in the tropics, I thought, watching my husband that afternoon with a can of dope in his hand, carefully sticking down the curling edges of fabric with his finger and paint brush. The heat, the salt moisture, the changes in temperature, all left their mark on the plane—those slow inroads of decay.

And not only on the plane, I felt, as the persistent banana smell of the dope drifted back to me (incongruously reminiscent of silver slippers being repainted for dancing school)—on oneself, too, there were inroads. There was the grit in hair, the torn hangnails on fingers, the cracked places on dry lips, and a general parched feeling all over one's body. I had a vague fear that if we stayed here much longer, we too would go under. Like everything else, we would be covered up. The dust would sift over us; and the rust imprison us also.

It was mid-afternoon. The jobs on the plane were nearly finished. My husband stood in a rowboat, with a can of orange paint, brushing over the dope and covering up the last patches. I climbed back into the cockpit, trying to be energetic. I repacked the baggage compartment, wrote up my diary, and recopied my radio notes. It was still early. All those isolated, repetitious acts strung one after another on the continuous threads of the blazing sun, the dust, the sigh of the wind, had not added up to make a day. The box was not more than half full.

There was nothing to do now but to face the thing we had been running away from all day. There was nothing left to do but to lie down and wait.

The quality of waiting, I thought wearily, as I rolled my coat under my head for a pillow, was always the same, no matter where it was; at an aviation field or a doctor's office; in a telephone booth or a garden; or even lying down in the baggage compartment of a plane, as I was now, staring at the barrel like ribs curving over my head. It was always the same. That broken-off detached piece of time, suspended in mid-air, hovering. Waiting, for the plane to come, for the door to open, for the bell to ring, for the hour to strike, for a message from Bathurst. Unable to fasten your attention on anything else, unable to rest. And yet, in that suspense, you grew so tired that you could rest your attention on any-thing—on the crushed-in side of an empty oil can, on strange advertisements of sanitary trusses in a magazine, on other people's telephone num-bers scrawled on dirty walls, "Main 1372—1372," on daddy longlegs clambering slowly and pain-fully over long grass, on the twisted pipes and wires at the back of the instrument board. You were so tired you could rest on any of these small and trivial items. You fastened on them desperately, straws on the surface in which you were suspended. You could put all your weight on them, the weight of a whole life—if only they would hold you. But they could not. Nothing could hold you except that one thing you were waiting for: the roar of a plane, the door opening, the bell ringing, the hour striking, the message from Bathurst.

Yes, here I was waiting again, as we had waited for the shackles in the machine shop, as I had waited for my husband rowing back from the sea, as we had waited for a change in the wind, for word from Dakar. The whole time on the island had been waiting, it seemed to me, lying there, staring at the ribbed fuselage, and holding all the different times in my mind like one load, one long inner pull. That had been behind everything, over everything we had done and felt here —that quality of suspense. That was the wave that climbed and climbed and never broke. That was the indrawn rising breath that never fell—like the wind.

Waiting was always like that, suspended, floating, unattached to life, up there somewhere in that long drawn-out sigh, beyond one's reach, like the wind. If only it could be pulled down, harnessed, rooted to life.

You tried to do it, of course, in all attempts

to pass the time away, in all attempts to fill up
the empty box as we had done today. Deny waiting; refuse to look at it. It was a vacuum, a waste
of time, a negative quality. But surely it was part
of life and that was not the answer.

Sometimes while I waited, I had tried to live
more intensely in the little things imprisoned
with me: in dusty blackberries, eternal in their
stillness by the side of a road; in weightily signifi-
cant sparrows pecking in the gravel; or sparkling
drops of dew in a field, blazing beyond their size.
But often there were no sparrows, no drops of
dew, only telephone numbers scribbled on walls,
only spokes of wheels, only gasoline pipes and
wires.

No, I supposed, waiting could only be linked
to life by accepting it, by seeing value in it for
itself. To wait, as the farmer after his crop is
planted, knowing there is nothing more he can
do, knowing that it now depends on things outside himself; but still, having faith in those
things, in the slow but inevitable process before
him.

To wait, as women wait for their children to
be born, happy in knowing that each second of
the time has meaning and purpose and is, because
of that, acceptable. This was the only waiting
which was really fruitful.

But how could one feel that way about this

time here? What connection could it have with me, now, lying on my back, staring up at the ribbed fuselage, at the twisted pipes and wires? If one could see ahead in time, as the farmer does; if one could see out through space, could one believe that this period was inevitable, too? That in this apparent vacuum something was growing; that even now, in this seemingly inactive period, all kinds of necessary things were proceeding at the fastest possible speed, rushing toward us. That what was happening in Bathurst, in telegraph offices, at official desks, in the streets, in the Health Department—all small events, everything was converging into the pattern of our lives? Perhaps something was ripening for us, even now—

CHAPTER XIV

"PLEASED TO GRANT . . ."

WE climbed up the hill for supper. As we paused and turned toward the bungalow, we saw a man hurrying down the path from the radio house—the "Chef." In his hand was a piece of yellow paper, fluttering in the wind. The radiogram, we both thought, and stood waiting for him, keeping our eyes on the yellow sheet as though we could guess its secret. We hardly looked at the "Chef." The piece of fluttering paper seemed so much the most vivid thing in the landscape at that moment, alive as a tongue of flame.

"Monsieur—for you—from Bathurst . . ." The "Chef" coughed breathlessly. My husband took the sheet from him without glancing up. We read it together, not moving, the even penciled words of the pale-faced operator: ". . . PLEASED TO GRANT AUTHORIZATION . . . KINDLY ADVISE TIME ARRIVAL . . ."

So, that's all there was to it—as simple as that—"Kindly advise time arrival"—as casual as that! Why did we worry? What was that nightmare we were caught in an hour ago? It had vanished, evaporated like the darkness of the night before. It was like waking from a bad dream, the relief, the peace, the weight dropped off your chest. Oh, it was only a dream—they didn't catch you—you're not going to be shot after all—it was only a dream.

It was like suddenly hearing the music of a procession after being deaf; after watching a marching band from a closed window, the baton waving aimlessly, the drumstick falling noiselessly, the rows of legs pacing in causeless rhythm. Then the window is opened and the sudden strains of music flood into the room, filling all those silent movements with life and meaning. The music had been out there all the time, only we had not heard it. Now the window is open, it is part of us. Now we tap our feet to it. It is beating in us.

I felt that life was beating again in us, pounding back into us like new blood. We were part of it again.

And happy, too, I felt no longer isolated, no longer outcast. "Pleased to grant authorization." Why, I thought, childishly pleased, they sound as if they might even want us. I felt some of the joy of a young and shy girl coming into a party full of strangers, terrified and alone, when someone, some lovely woman from that world of poised and sophisticated creatures, comes up to her and kisses her lightly, saying, "Why, my dear, how

nice to see you—" Oh, she thinks, dazzled, hesi-
tant, and happy, oh—they want me, is it possible
—they want me!

"Pleased to grant authorization," my husband
read again, an easy smile of relief on his face.
"Well, that's that." And he folded up the message
and tucked it casually in his pocket. That problem
was over, behind us. No need to worry any longer
about that. He had tucked it in his pocket and
forgotten about it. Other things to think about—
the take-off, how to manage that? When calmest,
in the morning? Where—below the point? Pretty
rough stretch of water—still—with a light load—
the sea went down at night a little—wind dropped
—early morning.

"Is it all right?" I said, watching the precious
slip of yellow paper disappear without a thought,
watching my husband's mind leap ahead to the
next problem.

"Oh, yes"—his voice was full and reassuring,
but he was still thinking of the swell outside the
harbor—"I think we can get off all right with a
light load."

We climbed the steps absent-mindedly into the
bungalow. The "Chef" came in quietly behind
us. I was still in a trance, "They want us—think
they want us!" My husband sat down at the table
without looking at it. He did not see the frayed
cloth, askew on the top, the solitary glass tooth-

pick stand, the bottles on the shelves, the wicker chair. The room had vanished. He was already far beyond the sea swell at the harbor entrance. He was at Bathurst. No trouble to get fuel, he was thinking, but that extra two hundred miles— Could we make it by day?—throttle down—fly by night? Heavy night take-off? The moon—yes, just in time to catch the moon, almost full—still had the moon—

The couple murmured quietly in the door. I watched my husband, trying to read the progress of his mind. Finally the "Chef" came over and pulled out his chair.

"You will go?" he asked mildly.

In spite of its quietness, the question jarred the silence.

"Go?" said my husband, startled from his thoughts. "Oh, yes, of course we'll go—we'll probably go in the morning if we can get off."

I looked up at their faces for the first time that evening, to find with a strange sense of shock that there was, of course, no change in them. They were just the same. No nightmare had ended for them, no burst of music after silence. Everything was just the same. Unmoved, they sat in their chairs facing us. There was an appalling stillness about them. Such stillness as I have only felt in a waiting train, standing in a country station. Another train moves by, clickety-click, clickety-click. The sound of rattling cars, the rush of wind, the kaleidoscopic pattern of passing faces and windows, light and darkness, give you the illusion that you too are moving. Then, with a last rattle and swish of wind, the train is gone. You are suddenly faced again with the same stark landscape; the still roadbed covered with oil and cinders, the still tracks, the still water tank, the telegraph poles, the ditch, the fence.

It was the same landscape I saw now in the faces opposite me. There was no flicker of movement in them; only a patient gaze followed the person speaking.

My husband continued his thoughts out loud, "The sea is quietest in the morning, isn't it?" He glanced across the table to those inert faces. "Doesn't the wind drop at night a little?"

"Oh, yes, Monsieur, a little—" (I had the impression of an old cart slowly pulling into jerky motion again.) The "Chef" bent himself seriously to my husband's question, "The wind drops a little at night, the sea too. It is best in the morning—"

There was another silence in which we ate our supper. After the plates were stacked to one side, the "Chef" leaned across the table and coughed in a half-apologetic, half-introductory fashion.

"Monsieur," he began earnestly, "will you take a letter for me to some company— Perhaps if they

put an airline through the Cape Verde Islands—
they might have need of a radio operator—"

"You want to change your job?" asked my
husband.

"Ah, yes," said the "Chef," shaking back a long
lock of hair, "I am looking for a new job. The
Company"—he lifted his eyebrows—"they have
two scales of wages, one for French and one for
natives—I am paid too little—"

He coughed again.

"And I cannot get a position in a government
station or on a boat, because I have not had the
training. One must have training and education
to get a government license—" He stood up and
went to the cupboard for his bottle of medicine.
"And I am too old—"

"How old are you?" asked my husband.

"Twenty-seven," he answered, stirring his medicine in a glass of water.

"How old is your wife?" I interrupted. I could
never guess. Sometimes she seemed to have lived
a long time; sometimes she was a child.

"She? She is sixteen—" He nodded in her direction carelessly and then went on, "And I am
married; I cannot live on that scale. If I could get
a position with an American company . . ." He
gulped down the glass of water.

"I'll take your letter," said my husband, "but
it's very doubtful that an American company will
come here."

"Ah, yes, Monsieur, I understand, but I have so little chance. I do not often see people. If you will be so kind—"

He took some loose sheets of lined paper from the shelf, and a bottle of violet ink and started to write.

My husband went out to find the mechanic and make arrangements about tomorrow's take-off. A few minutes later the "Chef" pushed back his chair, folded his sheet of paper in four, tucked it envelope-less into his inner pocket and hurried out.

The girl and I were left alone. She picked up the loose sheets of paper left lying on the bare table, shuffled them into a neat stack and then tucked them into a corner of the cupboard, weighting them down with the bottle of ink.

"You will start early?" she asked gently, half turning to me.

"Oh, yes," I said, stiffening to the old role of routine, "we always start early, when we fly, and tomorrow my husband is anxious to get off when the sea is quiet— But you needn't bother to get up—" I added as an afterthought, "We don't need . . ."

"Oh, yes—" she protested quickly, turning around and smiling at me, "we will have breakfast for you—before you go—" She picked up a stray pen from the table and turned back to the shelf with a little sigh, "C'est ennuyeux ici—all alone."

CHAPTER XV

THOSE TOWERS ON THE HILL

GOOD-BY—good-by!" but I was shouting at the empty air. Not even my husband in the next cockpit could hear me above the noise of the plane's engine, much less those tiny figures standing on the hill far below us. For we were in the air again, circling the little harbor, banking around on one wing, roaring our power arrogantly above the world we had just left. The bobbing chip-boat which had towed us out to sea, the neat square-box hangar, the crooked spider's-leg crane, the squat bungalow, the radio-tower needles pointing at the sky; all spun in review below us as we passed. For we were off.

What a take-off it had been—towed out of the choppy entrance, the Negro boys straining at the oars. That long taxi up and down the stretch of open water, the plane wallowing in the heavy swell. Would we ever get off such a sea? Then, facing the wind, warming up, and the long drive through the waves. The spray—the rush of water on the wings—up on the step—terrific whacks on the pontoons. Would they stand it? Something must crack. We're off—no—another spank—now, we're off—no—spank, spank. Something would break. He was stalling it. We're off—holding my breath for the next impact—which never came. We're off—then—we're off! Now climbing, turning, roaring up the steep air, we left the world that had imprisoned us a moment before.

How could it be the same world, I thought, looking down on it in amazement. It was so small, how could it hold anyone? That minute white shack under the radio towers—was that where we had been so discouraged when the message tapped out from Dakar? That narrow bungalow—was that where I sat bound in lethargy, in the armchair, night after night? The dust-colored thread curling up a gentle slope—was that the steep path I climbed so often to the bungalow? And those figures, those bobbing dots in the boat, those moving specks on the hill—were they the living people we had been talking to? The Frenchman, in his stained sweater and his sun helmet. The wide-smiling Negro boys who shuffled up to say good-by. The "Chef," drawing himself up to his lean height, buttoning his thin flapping coat, refusing to take any money for the trouble we had given him. "I am here chef—you are my guests—I cannot allow my guests to pay—" Finally he had taken enough for the radiograms only, protesting to the end that it was too much and he would send us what was left over. And that flutter of color, a tiny blur of yellow—that was the little girl, who had followed us about with a dusty box-camera. "You do not mind?" she had asked. "Plees?"

Only a few minutes ago—and now, although I was still shouting inaudible "good-bys" out of the back cockpit, and they were still waving their miniature arms from the hill, we were as separated as we would ever be. Space became time in that instant. We were as far away as we would be next week, next year, or at the end of life. They were now part of the past and—looking down on them was looking down at life from the altitude of death.

They would cease to be important to me, I realized, as the plane dipped first one wing and then another in a good-by salute. I did not want to—but I would forget them. They would be a dim and dreamlike memory, an old nightmare. Our plane, our eyes, and, now, our minds also would turn in another direction, toward Bathurst. Only one slight thread would hold us together a little longer. The radio—I remembered suddenly—those towers on the hill, the little hut with its one window to the sky, the pale operator with his eye on the clock. I must reel out the antenna and set the coils; I must establish contact.

"Darr dit darr, dit dit dit dit, darr dit darr dit - - - KHCAL [Our plane] CALLING CRKK [Porto Praia]."

PART 2

BATHURST

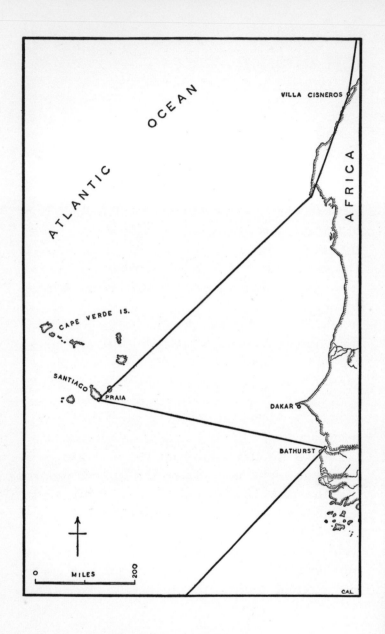

CHAPTER XVI

AND THE BRITISH

"ARRIVE BATHURST ABOUT 13:40 GMT." I tapped
a last message back to Porto Praia. The shore line
of Gambia was already rising, a dark ridge above
the colorless bright sea of mid-day. The point of
Dakar, that besieged city, was only a smudged
line on the horizon to our left. Our strange
islands were far behind; Bathurst was ahead.

It was flat from this distance, a long monotonous line, never rising to peaks or hills and taper-
ing only gradually on the edges, where sight began to blur, into the sea. I hardly knew where
it did taper, where it actually disappeared from
sight. It gave the impression of going on forever,
part of a huge curve, an immense continent.

Even as we drew nearer and made out sharper
lines that might be bluffs or cliffs, these were not
like the rocky sea-beaten coasts of Santiago. It
was unbelievably green, we began to notice, after
those bare volcanic hills, a thick sultry green
which seemed to emanate a kind of mist or heat
blur above the vegetation. Here a patch of green
was mottled indistinctly by barely perceptible

gradations of tone which set it off from the strips on either side. This mottled look, I knew, meant a town, the light masses of houses, the dark masses of trees—Bathurst. Soon we could distinguish the softly irregular line of palms and the unyielding profile of buildings sticking up between them. The points of masts, the blocks of piers began to show as if floating on the sea.

It was a big place, then, Bathurst. A British colony, of course. We would be all right here. The mouth of the river, now I could make out the two points that marked the entrance, was broad and spacious like a big bay. No trouble taking off that. It was full of little sailing boats, dinghies and two-masted yawls, safely sheltered in its wide expanse. Some bigger schooners hugged the wharves which lined one side of the town. Lots of boats—traffic—I thought with relief, remembering the deserted harbor at Santiago.

The water was still and peaceful, hundreds of little ripples breaking up its muddy surface. No trouble landing there. We circled the white-stoned town, the flags, the masts, the ships and docks, the dense green mangrove shores, and landed gently, cutting the water with an imperceptible clip across the brown ripples. Perfect landing, I thought, as I wrote down the log, "Landed Bathurst 13:58 GMT." How different from the spanks off Santiago!

The engine puttered on gently as we nosed toward a marked buoy. I put away the log books, closed up the radio set, and raised myself up in the cockpit. It was incredibly hot, steaming— much hotter than Porto Praia—damp and sultry, not a breath of wind. Those muddy ripples on the water must be from tide—no wind at all. That was good, though; we wouldn't be long tying up.

A small trim motorboat was cutting circles around our plane. Officers in white uniforms stood up, waved their sun helmets at us. "His Excellency the Governor asked us . . ." "His Excellency's car . . ." Quickly and quietly we were tied up to a buoy, helped down into the boat, and headed off to the pier.

"You know, Colonel Lindbergh," said one of the officers, looking at us with genuine concern, "you two really ought to wear sun helmets."

"Yes, but we're used to the sun," answered my husband at the blaze of white-topped heads in the boat with us, "and we get some protection from these flying helmets."

"Ah—but it's the back of the neck—there's where it gets you, you know. You have no shade there at all—"

"But we're not in the sun for long," countered my husband.

"Oh—you'd be surprised—strikes you down as quick as that—" The officer snapped his fingers.

"How about a straw hat?" pursued my husband, thinking of the bulky unfoldable helmets.

"Not nearly so good," said the officer authoritatively, "you see, these are cork-lined—there's a special property that—ah—cuts out the rays." He took off his sun helmet, drummed on it sharply with his fingernails, and clapped it back on his head. "We'll get you some in the store."

Here we are again, I thought, sinking back into the atmosphere comfortably, with the English taking care of us. How they love to take care of people. Somebody was trying to help me up onto the pier.

"Thank you, I don't really need . . ."

A covered car was waiting for us in the shade of a silk-cotton tree. Just one blazing stretch of pavement to cross before we reached its cool shelter. The seats were lined with immaculate white strips of cloth. We sank back in ease.

"His Excellency's car—you are going straight to Government House—the Governor is away, but the acting Governor and his wife have asked you to stay with them." The officer shut the door.

"Are you sure it is quite convenient?" we protested. "We don't need to . . ."

"Oh, yes—wouldn't hear of anything else—His Excellency said you were to—they're waiting for you—"

"But it is very late," I argued, "after lunch—I

hope they're not waiting—perhaps there is a hotel—"

"Oh, no—don't think about it—it's all arranged."

We started off smoothly. I hoped it was all right. No use arguing. They liked taking care of people. I supposed that was why their colonies were so well run—this sort of thing now. We were driving down well-paved streets lined by freshly whitewashed houses with tin roofs and green shutters. Cement posts and walls marked off the lots. Telephone wires ran ahead of us. Trees, evenly spaced, shaded the sidewalks. Neat brick gutters were swept and clean. Carts and cars, and people on bicycles, filled the road, keeping well to the left. A steady stream of natives padded the sidewalks in bare feet; Negro women in wide calico skirts, children strapped to their backs, and baskets on their heads; Negro men, with their European shirts hanging outside like tunics; men in sun helmets, in fezzes, in large straw basket-hats; women with only cloth skirts around the hips and bandannas on their heads— all jostling and hurrying along the sidewalks, as if they had some work to finish or some place to go. Life was going on here; it meant something. Time counted; we were in the stream again. It was an orderly life, too. Policemen in white uniforms and sun helmets stood on the corners. Here was a wide-spreading silk-cotton tree that people gathered about as a village green. Here was a fenced-off cricket ground, a grandstand, a British flag. It all breathed of peace, order, and security. I remarked on this fact.

"It certainly feels good to get onto British territory," agreed my husband cheerfully.

There was no flicker on the face of the white-helmeted officer. Maybe he hadn't heard, I thought. Or perhaps it was modesty? I stole a glance under the helmet. No, I realized, not modesty—just boredom. And I made a mental note not to make remarks like that to the British. A little stupid, they think them. So obvious!

We drove between the wide gates of Government House; past the native guards, pacing their beat in khaki uniforms with red vests and fezzes; past feather-duster palms and dripping Bougainvillea. The Governor stood in the door, a saluting guard beside him. His wife came down a flight of broad stone steps to greet us. She looked cool and lovely in a thin dress of lavender voile. Her dress, her gestures, and her voice all called up another world. They breathed of English summers. I was sure there were rose-beds and Delphinium in a garden behind her and tea on the lawn and no weightier problems than a few friendly wasps in the jam-pot. I looked at her in astonished admiration.

She held out her hand. "You must come in and have some lunch," she said in her soft English voice. "I hope it is all right—we didn't know quite when you were coming." She smiled apologetically. "I am afraid the fish is a little overdone."

"Oh," I said, speechless with confusion, "thank you so much—I am sure—" I could not say anything more. It would be impossible to tell her how grateful I felt at that moment ("They want us—think! They want us.")—as impossible as trying to explain how strange it seemed to be back in a world where it mattered when the fish was "a little overdone."

We were taken through shuttered verandas, high-ceilinged halls, up a flight of steps to a glistening white bedroom. White mosquito nets were draped chastely over turned-down linen sheets. There was a pitcher of barley water on the bedside table, hot water in the bathroom and soap that smelled of lavender. (How blissful—a hot bath!)

We came down to lunch. Negro servants in white coats glided noiselessly in and out the curtained doors. The table was set with gleaming silver and glass. The food was delicious.

After lunch we had a bath; we had a rest between the cool linen sheets. We went out for a drive to the flying field. A flight of British planes had just come across Africa from the Sudan. Some of the officers came back to Government House for dinner. We exchanged notes on our trips. They minimized the difficulties of a trip across Africa; we spoke lightly of the rollers off Santiago. We felt part of a large brotherhood of people who fly. They had just come from Egypt; we were going to Brazil. It was all very jolly—flying was easy.

Before going to bed we walked out under the palms, across a road to the pier that stretched out into the harbor. It was clear and beautiful. The moon, not yet fully up, lit a path across the barely perceptible ripples on the bay. Smooth and still and peaceful. No wind, thank goodness—that sound had stopped at last. We stood at the edge of the pier where a light glowed softly over some steps which led down to the water.

A large fish flicked in the water below us, breaking its satin surface.

"Look," we said, startled, "the fish!"

"Oh, yes," explained the Governor, "they seem to come here at night, attracted by the light, I suppose. We often stay and watch them."

A silver fin flicked again in the light, making little ripples lap in cadence against the steps. How magical, I thought, like the fairy-tale of the fisherman and the flounder.

Flounder, flounder in the sea,
Prithee hearken unto me—

(What was the rest of it?)

I come to beg a boon of thee

"A boon of thee"—that was it. And then the flounder rose out of the sea and granted the fisherman any wish he might desire. I would wish— No, I stopped myself, I wouldn't think about wishes tonight. I wouldn't think about the future at all. We had left Porto Praia; we were safe in Bathurst. Tomorrow was time enough to think about our problems.

We turned and walked slowly back along the pier, our footsteps knocking clearly through the still air.

CHAPTER XVII

PIECES OF A PUZZLE

THE next morning we began to wrestle with the problems of a South Atlantic crossing. And as we talked back and forth, we went into another world, turned inward to our minds and lived in a landscape made of the shoals and rocks and shifting tides of our difficulties. How should we plan our course among them and reach the point we were aiming for? What alternative paths were open to us and what obstacles lay in their way?

At times it seemed to me we were struggling with a gigantic Chinese puzzle. Some of the pieces were fixed; some were movable, and we must fit them all into a smooth whole. There were the known and immovable factors of the plane, such as its wing area, its horsepower, the buoyancy and shape of the pontoons. Contrasted against these were the known and movable factors, somewhat under our control, such as its cruising speed, range, and weight of equipment. Then there were the known and immovable circumstances of place; the harbors of Bathurst and Natal, and the distance of ocean between. Then again there were the known and uncontrollable conditions of light and darkness; the length of the day and the night; the moon, its waxing and waning, its time of rising and setting. And finally, most difficult part of the puzzle, we must reckon with the unknown and uncontrollable elements of wind and weather.

All must be fitted in together to one aim, our crossing of the Atlantic. There must be some way to do it easily. ("Don't use force—they all slip in easily, once you know the combination," says the Almighty being who hands you the separate pieces.) And sometimes the chief difficulty seemed to be holding all the pieces in your hands at the same moment. If only you could see them all clearly at once it would not be hard to make the pattern correctly.

But you never could. You started out bravely saying, "If we take off at daybreak—" And a voice interrupted, "But the moon rises later every night—" (Try another piece then.) "If we take off in the evening—" you said. And a voice parried, "But a forced landing at night on the Atlantic—?" Back and forth, went the pieces in our fingers; take-off—landing, daybreak—sunset, range—weight, time—speed, light—darkness, moonrise—moonset. Would we ever get them balanced, fitted in their places, each separate piece holding its exact and destined position, pushed just the right amount but not too far, nothing forced, nothing cracked or broken, a harmonious whole?

A giant's cat's-cradle it seemed to me at times, the thread in our hands wound in and out about our fingers. Some of the loops must remain taut on our fingers; others we could play with, holding them precisely, pairing them exactly, doubling them back and forth, in and out, to make the pattern. But if our fingers slipped and lost a single thread, if one loop were forgotten, the whole intricate taut structure, so rigidly shaped at one moment, could, in the next, shatter its form completely and ravel out into a meaningless piece of tangled thread.

For the problem of a flight from Bathurst was far more difficult than one from Porto Praia. The extra two hundred miles of ocean made a great difference to our calculations. It meant that we could not complete the entire trip by daylight at our normal cruising speed.

("And if we push the engine?"

"Well—then perhaps, but . . ." The argument started.)

We could, of course, fly fifteen or twenty knots faster but it would be a greater strain on the engine and we would need much more fuel for the flight. In fact we would need so much fuel at that speed that we might not be able to take off the water with the load.

("The take-off, you see—we're already overloaded . . .")

At best we would reach the other side a very
short time before sunset with an uncomfortably
low reserve of gasoline.

("And if we have head winds . . . ?"

"Or storms, or fog . . .")

If we had bad weather and were forced to de-
tour, we would reach the South American coast
after darkness anyway, and might even run out
of fuel while we were still over the ocean.

("Forced landing at sea—?")

Apparently there were too many uncertain factors in a daylight flight. Our reserves were not
great enough in time, light, fuel, and general
safety. The margin was too close.

("—type of flying I don't like to do—")

Actually, the speed for greatest fuel economy
was about a hundred knots. At that rate, it would
take us sixteen hours to reach Natal.

("Only about twelve hours of daylight here—"

"We can't make it then—we'll have to fly at
night.")

Reluctantly we gave up the idea of a dawn to
dusk flight, in spite of the advantages of daylight
and shorter hours. Part of the trip would have to
be by night.

("Night flight, then—but the take-off?")

There were three possibilities open to us. We

could leave at night and arrive in daylight. We could leave in daylight and arrive at night. Or we could leave in the evening, fly through the night, and arrive in the early morning. Each possibility had its advantages and disadvantages which must be weighed carefully, one against the other.

There were, of course, no night-flying facilities at Bathurst or Natal, but we had a full moon which would make either a night landing or take-off feasible.

("But the moon will start to wane . . .")

Tomorrow the moon would be full, but each day after that would mean less light. We must leave soon or we would have no moon at all. Within three or four days, even, it would be of little use to us.

("If we take off at daybreak—")

We could take off in the morning, but then we would have to locate our position at night on the South American coast, and to make a night landing in a completely unknown harbor.

("And the moon might be covered by clouds when we get there . . .")

Even though the weather was usually good along the Brazilian coast, and we would be in constant touch with the Pan American radio stations, it seemed unsafe to count too definitely on having a clear sky sixteen hours after we left.

("If the weather is bad . . . ?")

Up to the time we were about halfway across we could turn back if we got word that the sky was clouding over. But after that? We might be able to reach Fernando de Noronha, a small island, two hundred miles northeast of the Brazilian coast. If not, we would have to land in open ocean before sunset, or change our course to St. Paul's Rocks, about six hundred miles northeast of Natal, and land in the large ocean swells on the sheltered side.

("But there is another complication, the moon rises later every night—")

Tonight the moon would rise at five o'clock, and would take several hours before it was high enough to outline distinctly objects on the ground. Tomorrow night it would rise almost an hour later and would continue to lose nearly an hour each day. Even if we left immediately there would be a period of darkness between sunset and moonlight at the end of our flight.

("If we take off at night, then?")

We could take off after midnight, by moonlight, from the harbor at Bathurst. In this case, we would arrive on the other side several hours before dark, and could find our position and make our landing in good light. This would be a definite advantage. The harbor of Bathurst, also, was now familiar to us and we could look over it carefully before taking off.

("But an overload take-off—and only the light of the moon?")

There was not much to choose between a night take-off and a night landing. Both were difficult. The simplest plan seemed to be an all night flight. This would let us take off with our overload in full daylight. We would also have a short period of flying before dark, after we left Bathurst, during which we could still return and make a daylight landing if everything were not going well. During the night flight itself we would have the stars for navigation. ("Arcturus—Aldebaran—Alpheratz"—how often I had said them over in my mind, like an incantation.)

They would give us a much more definite position than using the sun by day. With our bubble-sextant, on a clear night, we could always get lines of position from two navigation stars and, at their intersection, find our exact location. By day, with the sun alone to use, we could only get one line, a huge curve on which, by dead reckoning, we assumed our position.

By night, also, we would undoubtedly have much longer range for our radio. A wave with a daylight range of 0 to 450 miles, jumped at night to a range of 300 to 2,200 miles. A wave with a day-time range of 0 to 600 miles, reached at night a range of 400 to 3,500 miles. It would be an immense advantage for us to be in contact, from the beginning, with the Pan American stations on the Brazilian coast, 1,800 miles or more away.

("And if our engine fails at night?")

We might, of course, have to make a night landing in the open Atlantic. But with the reliability of modern engines there was not much chance of failure. If worst came to worst and we had to make a forced landing, we carried three parachute flares which would probably give us enough light to get down without serious damage.

("Night flight, then? . . ."

"Yes—night flight . . .")

We would leave in the evening and fly into dawn. That was settled then. We stopped our discussions. We put all other problems out of our minds. Night flight—we could start to work on that basis.

A long message went off to Pan American Airways: "PLEASE SEND DAILY BEGINNING SATURDAY WEATHER FORECAST BETWEEN PERNAMBUCO PARA ALSO OVER ATLANTIC . . . PARTICULARLY INTERESTED FOG LARGE STORMS HEAD WINDS . . . PROBABLY START 18:00 GREENWICH . . . TRANSMITTING HOUR AND HALF HOUR . . . LINDBERGH."

We went to the store, guided by our English friend, and bought sun helmets. My husband went off to inspect the plane and to refuel. He was gone all the afternoon. In the evening he came back for dinner. We sat again at the Governor's table. The lights burned softly, the conversation was gay. The officers from the air-field were there. We toasted the King.

After supper my husband turned to the Governor. "You know," he said, "there isn't a breath of wind in the harbor this evening—dead calm— absolute glass water. We'd never get off a surface like that, with our load." He hesitated and smiled. "The Captain of the Port seemed to think it usually was like that here in the evenings. Would you agree to that, Sir?"

"Evening—late afternoon?" The Governor paused a moment. "Why, yes, it's the stillest time in the day this season. Hardly ever any wind— wouldn't you say so?" He turned to his aide for corroboration.

"Yes, Sir"—the aide bent forward authoritatively—"as a rule, the wind dies down after three —never any wind in the evening this time of year—no wind at all."

No wind in the evening.

"Oh—" said my husband, with a half-smile and a shrug of the shoulders. The Chinese puzzle seemed again to fall to pieces in our hands. For a few minutes we had been off our guard.

We had forgotten the wind.

CHAPTER XVIII

LINES OF DEFENSE

"WELL, when *is* there a wind?" asked my husband.

"In the morning, I should say," was the answer.

"Just about sunrise, you get a wind, invariably," pronounced an officer.

"Yes—that's true," said another, "there's always a morning breeze. It gradually dies down in the heat of the day."

"Well—we may have to go in the morning," said my husband; "we've got a pretty heavy load. We can't take off from glass water—have to have *some* wind. We had too much at Santiago."

"Oh, you would never get that here—never—"

"Not in the harbor, no—"

"You think we're more likely not to have *any* wind?" questioned my husband.

"Oh, I think you'll get a good breeze in the morning—at daybreak, that is."

"That's probably the time to go, then."

We went to bed with our minds working over a new set of plans. A daybreak take-off meant a night landing, we knew that. But if we got off with a good load of fuel (my husband worked with pencil and paper), we could cruise fast enough to make Fernando de Noronha before dusk, and still have range enough to wait until the moon was well up before landing.

The moon would be full (we got out the Almanac) tomorrow night, December second. We could not be ready as soon as that. One day, at least, we would need for preparation. The day after, December third (we turned the pages of the Almanac), the moon rose about six-thirty at Natal. By nine it would be giving a fair light. The later we were, the more light we would have for landing. We would be flying all the time into better conditions, plunging deeper not into day, but into brighter and brighter moonlight.

"If we got off with a good load of fuel"—our plans always started like this, prefaced with an "if." They rose towering one on the other, like "the house that Jack built." It all depended on the first "if": "if we had range," "if we got off with a good load of fuel," "if we had a wind," "if the weather were clear."

Take-off and landing, wind and weather—the problems were still there. We could never quite settle them. We went to bed still juggling with them and woke the next morning to find them in exactly the same place, like the dolls one left

as a child, in frozen disarray all night in a corner
of the nursery.

Take-off and landing, wind—I sat up in bed and
looked out of the window. It was cool and fresh.
The tops of the palms in Government House
gardens were moving gently on the skyline, the
long stiff feather-duster branches flattening
against each other. There was certainly a wind.

"Look, there's a wind!"

"Yes, and there'll be more out in the bay. They
must be right about the morning breeze."

"It's eight o'clock now, too; it was probably
stronger at daybreak."

After breakfast we received an answer from
our cable to Pan American asking for weather
reports. "WEATHER PERNAMBUCO PARA ALWAYS
GOOD NEVER FOG . . ."

"Well, that simplifies things," said my husband
cheerfully, "but we mustn't count on it too much.
The chances are we'll have a clear sky for landing
—and we could land at Fernando de Noronha,
before dark, if we get a bad report ahead. Yes—
that settles it."

"We'll leave tomorrow, then?"

"Tomorrow morning. I'll go down to the bay
and get everything ready."

There was a full day's work on the plane. The
refueling alone would take a good part of the

morning, for we were putting in more gasoline than we had ever carried before. "We can always take some of it out," my husband said, "if we can't get off the water—but we might as well try." The extra reserve of fuel could be translated into light, time, and safety, at the other end. ("Fernando de Noronha before dark"—"Range enough to fly into bright moonlight.")

Then there was the general overall check of the plane and engine before a long flight, and, of course, the endless recurring battle against the ravages of salt water and a tropical sun. The pontoons again had to be pumped out. There were new places where the fabric was peeling off the wings. Some of the aluminum fittings and steel cables were showing more signs of corrosion.

I went down to arrange radio schedules, with the station at Bathurst, and sent a message to Porto Praia asking them to be "on watch" for us. ("WE LISTEN YOU ALL TIME," said Porto Praia.)

In the evening my husband came back, carrying equipment he had taken out of the plane to lighten our load. For we had not only extra fuel to carry on this flight, but extra water in case of a forced landing at sea.

"These are all things we won't need," he said, dumping the load in an incongruous pile on the floor of our bedroom.

There was a large white roll of charts of the

African coast, the Azores, the Canaries, and the Cape Verde Islands. We could leave these behind. Then there were our Greenland sealskin kamiks (boots) and a parka hood. Two pairs of rubber boots stood up stiffly side by side. We had not used them much on this trip, except in the north. They were only an extra convenience for working around the plane in shallow water. We could discard them, also. In the tropics it did not matter so much if your feet got wet.

"We won't need these any more, either," said my husband, coming in with another load. He lined up a row of cans on the floor before me; tetraethyl lead, and magneto oil, pontoon cement, dope, paint, fabric for wing patches, and the aluminum bucket. We would not be refueling on the ocean or doing any repair work. It would be much too rough.

"Aren't you taking the anchor?" I asked, seeing it lying in a nest of coiled chain and rope in the corner.

"No, we can get another on the other side," said my husband, "we've still got a canvas bag to use in an emergency. If we land near shore we can fill it up with rocks or mud. And that," he added, pointing to our small anchor and rope, "weighs thirty-seven pounds. That's over thirty miles in fuel," he figured out, "or almost four gallons of water and canteens."

Water, on a flight like this, is the heaviest item of the emergency provisions, and perhaps the most vital. There is no satisfactory way either to cut down on its weight or to use a lighter substitute. It was a very different problem in Greenland where we could always get water from the snow or from streams, and where, in consequence, we had not carried as much. Instead we had laid in a stock of concentrated foods which were now almost useless to us. My husband had brought some of these back from the plane with him, neatly labeled tins which he stacked up on the floor, baked beans, soup cubes, and chocolate rations. When you are out in a rubber boat in the middle of a tropical sea you do not want a lot of dry food which makes you thirsty. You need more water and less to eat.

"How much water have we got?" I asked.

"Eight gallons."

"And food?"

"Food enough for several weeks, but not food you have to cook. Pretty difficult to set up a Primus stove in a rubber boat on the sea. I haven't cut down on any of our reserves"—he began checking items on his equipment lists— "just taking out dry rations and things we don't need."

I began to realize more vividly than ever before what those lists of my husband meant; those impressive itemized pages labeled "Airplane and Engine Equipment," "Radio Equipment," "Emergency Radio Equipment," "Navigation Equipment," "Emergency Equipment for Forced Landing at Sea," "Emergency Equipment for Forced Landing on Land," "Emergency Provisions." I had seen the countless objects themselves, sorted out, appraised, and weighed, before the trip had begun. I had watched them on our bedroom floor at home, marveled impersonally at each surprising detail: "He's even got fishhooks— '27 fishhooks—1 oz.,' " or "He's even weighed the needles and thread."

But it was a detached and almost literary admiration, as one marveled, reading *Swiss Family Robinson*, at the number of useful articles that came out of Mother Robinson's bag on the desert island. It was quite different perusing the lists now, on the eve of a transoceanic flight, when tomorrow we might be depending on them for our lives.

For all these items, I realized with a warm feeling of confidence, carefully weighed and precisely noted down, added together to make our reserves. Bit by bit they built up our walls of defense, ramparts encircling us. The first line of defense consisted of our flying reserves, things which one counted on almost without thinking: extra fuel, navigation instruments, our radio, our

sextant, our gyroscopes for blind flying—all of
which should keep us from having a forced landing.

But if something went wrong in this first line,
there was another to fall back on. We had reserves
in case of a forced landing at sea, especially if the
plane were not damaged. Planes had landed in
open ocean before and stayed afloat for many
days. In this case we would still have our regular
plane's radio. (We had often used it successfully
from the water by stretching the antenna out
along the wing.) We had food and water for several weeks and we would have, of course, all our
navigation equipment.

And if this second line were broken through, if
the plane were damaged on landing, we still had
a final, inner reserve. Besides our food and water,
our sextant and our navigation equipment, we
had a rubber boat with oars, sails, and storm top.
We had our completely separate emergency radio
set. This inconspicuous black box, stowed away
in the baggage compartment, seemed to me as
wonderful as any Aladdin's lamp. It was, when
closed, waterproof and crashproof. It could float
and had been dropped from a hangar roof during
its tests.

Or, if we came down on land, there was another
group of emergency equipment: a bug-proof tent,
among other things, a medical kit, a revolver and

ammunition—altogether a store that would have warmed the heart of Father Robinson and his sons.

But he had taken nothing from our reserves, he said. The walls were still intact around us. The lists were checked, the equipment packed away carefully in the baggage compartment of the plane. We were ready to go.

"When will we leave?" I asked, putting the rest of my things into my blanket-roll bundle that evening.

"Let's see," said my husband, "we must be out on the water, ready to take off, before sunrise." (Not one drop of daylight must be spilled if we were to make Fernando de Noronha before dark.) "All set to go at five-thirty, say"—my husband began to count back from there in his mind— "about an hour's work on the plane, that's four-thirty, half an hour to get out to the plane from here, four—we should leave here at four—get up at three-thirty. We'd better get to bed; it's nine-thirty now."

We said good-by to the Governor and his wife. "You must have something hot before you go," she insisted. "I will have coffee put up in a thermos for you, and sandwiches—and something for the trip, as well."

Then at last, when we turned out the light on the silhouettes of our discarded equipment, our rubber boots and our soup tins, on the thermos bottle and the alarm clock on the bedside table—then, falling back in bed, I forgot those endless lists of equipment, those reserves tucked away in the plane. I no longer thought about the trip tomorrow, its problems or its hazards. I no longer thought about the day of preparation behind us. The cover of the mind had gone down like the lid of a trunk. Even the last unruly odds and ends, "Did I pack the pencils"—"Is there anything left in the cupboard," were closed in.

All thoughts were covered under the incoming tide of finality in my mind. Only certain rocks remained above water for me to rest on for a moment, certain flashing pictures from the day's events that were pleasant to dwell on; the Governor's smile as he toasted our success at dinner that night, his wife's voice saying, "You must have something hot before you go." Then these, too, were swept away. The surface of the mind was an even sea.

All that remained was that familiar indefinable lump in the chest. It had nothing to do with problems or perplexities. It did not seem specifically related to anything. It was simply the going-away lump, that had been there when I was a child and was as uncontrollable now as then. Leaving the seaside after the summer was over; leaving home for the seaside; leaving houses,

country and city, casual and important, temporary and permanent—any place that you had made
with difficulty and affection your home. In fact,
simply going away.

Why, I sometimes argued with myself, you
might be your great-great-grandmother, who
never left her New England house or village, instead of someone who traveled constantly. What
did they call it in New England when they felt
this same thing, this lump in the throat, this sick
feeling in the pit of the stomach, when the trunks
were strapped up and the hat boxes were piled
high at the front door, waiting for the carriage?
"Journey-proud," they said. "She's just journey-
proud."

That was all it was, I said to myself, and, having
defined it, felt comforted, as if, now it had a label,
it too could be stowed away, packed up in its
proper place along with the rest of the equipment, the rubber boat and the bug-proof tent.
"Just journey-proud, that's all," I said to myself
and went to sleep.

CHAPTER XIX

OUR EARLY MORNINGS

BANG, bang, bang. Someone was knocking on the door. Out of the soft depths of a new-mown sleep I woke, confused and complaining. Pitch black, the middle of the night. But something was wrong. We were to have a sleep, a night's sleep.

"Time to get up." My husband switched on the light.

But the night, was it over? I felt cheated. Yes, it must be over. I could tell by the stretched feeling around my eyes. I had slept. The night had gone.

My husband was already out of bed. I remembered now, they were calling us. We were getting up early to fly. This was the morning we were going across the Atlantic to South America.

I rose like an automaton and started to dress hurriedly, the lethargic sleepy person on top urged on by some blind feeling of urgency underneath, a voice hammering through to me like the man knocking on the door, and explaining, "Yesterday, when you were awake, you decided to do this. It was very important. When you are more awake you will know why."

And gradually as I dressed, my eye on the clock, I began to feel the importance of what I was doing. Twenty minutes of—leave the house at four—be ready at ten of, upstairs—must not be late—all set to go before the sun rises. The light, the precious light, must not be wasted.

Outside, the night was still a rich deep black. No hint of day had broken through its thickly piled surface. Safe, safe—we were still safely covered by the dark. We had time to get everything ready, everything set, before the surface wore thin.

The weather? Clear, as far as we could see. There were stars, and the moon, not yet set, still gave a little light. Wind? We peered out of the window at the dim outlines of palm trees against the black sky, straining our eyes to catch some change in their blurred profiles. Yes—their shapes changed from time to time; they were moving. Yes—there was a wind. Good, a wind!

I put on my flying clothes. What a relief to be back in the routine again. All this was easy now. No lump in the chest this morning; no "journey-proud" feeling. That was behind. Nothing but action lay ahead, the swift day; and my part to take in it was clear. ("Did you wind the chro-

nometers?" "Here are some extra pencils.") No
space for doubt or hesitation.

Besides, this was our regular life—getting up
early in the morning to fly. ("Ssh"—what a noise
the thermos made, set down on the table.) A
summer of early mornings, dark, hushed, and
hurried, lay behind us. No matter how much our
stopping places differed, our exits from them were
always the same. Out of a Greenland cottage, or
a European hotel; from an embassy, or a desert
fort, it made no difference. We woke in the dark,
confused and uncertain. We dressed hurriedly in
the silence of other people's sleep, fumbling
on the floor for our shoes. ("Listen—you'll wake
up the house—how the boards squeak.") We stole
out noiselessly, in our old clothes again, as we
had come, shouldering our bundles. Out into the
air, back to our own life, flying. Only that was
real, then. Everything else—sitting around at dinner tables, meeting people, watching, waiting,
filling up the time—was unreal. Our life began
again with these exits.

Further back than the summer, too, early mornings were ours. At home, in Maine, on Long
Island, on the West Coast, always getting up early
to catch the first light for flying, to get to our
destination before dark, to seize the world when
it was fresh and new, when no one else was about

—no one except those few other early morning guardians.

For the world has different owners at sunrise. Fields belong to hired men opening gates for cows; meadows, to old women with carpetbags, collecting mushrooms. Even your own garden does not belong to you. Rabbits and blackbirds have the lawns; a tortoise-shell cat who never appears in the daytime patrols the brick walks, and a golden-tailed pheasant glints his way through the iris spears.

To seize the world then is to have a new one. There is an element of discovery in it, of adventure and plunder. And for flyers it is more than plunder of a new world, but of time itself, priceless hours, snatched from the morning, stored up for use at the end of the day.

This time we were stealing now, from the night, I realized, would be made good to us. It was only night we were spending, a dark and faceless coin. It would be paid back to us in the clear gold of daylight at the other end, in the pure silver of moonlight. (Fernando de Noronha before dark—range enough to fly into bright moonlight.)

"Hurry—it's ten of—are you ready?" Hurry but don't make a sound. "Ssh—you will wake up the house." The squeak of an opened drawer—the rattle of paper. Whispers. "Give me a hand on the cloth and I'll tie up the bundles." Even the rope squeaked under my fingers, tying the knot, and the bundle thumped on the floor as I turned it. "Listen, there are steps in the hall—they've come for the bags—are you ready?" "All right— they're all in a pile—I'll carry the helmet and maps." A knock on the door.

The two Negro servants, immaculate even at this hour in their long sashed coats, shouldered our bundles carefully, the blanket rolls, our canteens, and the white canvas sack. "Be careful of that one, will you? It has instruments in it." You could never carry anything, I remembered, in a British colony. A last glance at our room—nothing left? I had the helmets, our lunch, the maps, and the radio bag of papers. "No, thank you, I *always* carry this." My husband had some canteens, and the camera. No, nothing left except our discarded equipment—the boots, and the anchor staring at us reproachfully from their neat pile on the floor. Someone would come for those and ship them home after us. We turned out the light and started off, our rubber-soled shoes squeaking down the halls after the silent bare feet of the Negroes.

At the bottom of the stairs we met the Governor and his wife. They had got up to see us off. "At four o'clock—how could you?" "Good-by— good-by." They seemed really concerned about us. We talked in whispers, not that there were people to wake but instinctively, as though by common consent not to shatter the strange sacredness of early-morning stillness. "Thank you so much—"as if we could really thank them! One can never thank people, I thought regretfully, at least not by piling gratitude on top of them like heavy American Beauty roses. One can never pay in gratitude; one can only pay "in kind" somewhere else in life. Unconsciously, perhaps, some day without knowing it, one might give by a simple ordinary act—as they had given to us. "Thank you— Good-by—"

Out through the sheltered verandas and down the wide steps of Government House again. It was just a day or two ago we had climbed up them with a feeling of relief and of homecoming, with the sense of something accomplished, and of ordeals behind us. Now, everything lay ahead. Everything was yet to be proved and accomplished, today—tonight. We stacked our baggage in the open car. "The big one—the little one— there—be very careful of that one, will you? It has instruments in it. Look out—I said *be very careful of that one.* Put it on top—please."

The car lurched; we started off. I waved— "Good-by—" Did I have everything? The maps —yes, on my lap. The radio bag—yes, on top. The sun helmet—yes. The lunch—yes, tucked inside. Maps, radio bag, sun helmet, lunch.

Out of the gates of Government House, past the dim cricket field, the black shadowed silk-cotton trees; down the dark streets, wide open, swept clean of any life except our own. And we, in the midst of all this death-like stillness, seemed, even at our mild speed of twenty miles an hour, recklessly alive; tearing through empty streets, devoid of motion; racing noisily around corners, hushed of sound. Surely we would shatter the stillness and startle into life the blank faces of these sheltered houses. People would stir in bed and wonder what madmen were about that hour of the night—while we had left another stopping place behind, another exit. Another day's flight had begun.

CHAPTER XX

"IF WE TAKE OFF AT DAYBREAK—"

WE drew up to the closed gates of the dock-yard. A lantern dangled on one of the bars. The driver honked the horn cautiously, startling the silence. After a minute, a sleepy guard shuffled up, unlocked the gates and swung them back slowly. We drove in over the uneven cinder-surfaced ground. The pier stretched ahead of us, a small light on its far end. In the dim moonlight beyond, we could see the black outline of the plane, the mooring lantern swinging above the hump of the engine cowling. We climbed out of the car with our bundles and went down to the end of the pier where there was a ladder. Some-one whistled across the water to the native guards in a rowboat. Oars splashed in the silence; the boat lantern flickered. They came up to the dock.

"Here—our bundles—the big one first, please—there—the little one—the white bag—be careful of that one, will you? Put it on the back seat—I'll hold it."

We started off across the water. It was still dark. Only the moonlight here and there showed up the surface in silver patches. Slightly ruffled, but not much wind, I thought, gauging the size of the ripples. There would be more, probably, out in the bay.

We pushed up to the pontoons, I putting out my hand to hold off the boat and keep it from bumping against the side. My husband jumped out. One end of the pontoon sank under his weight, the water rippling up over the top. "Give me the bags—will you—the big one first—" He piled them on the wing gingerly, then pulled out the sliding steel tubes that made steps on the side of the round fuselage. Stepping up on one, he slid back the cockpit covers which were damp with dew. I handed up the maps, the radio bag, the helmet, and the lunch. He dumped them in the rear cockpit.

Now I could get out. Left, right, left—the swing up into my cockpit. Everything all right? I felt with my hands in the dark. The driftmeter was still covered with the helmet as I left it, to keep out dust and damp. The radio key was at my right hand. The coil box at my feet was closed. The transmitter door in front of me was tightly screwed shut. The antenna reel on my left was wound up and the brake on. All right. I shoved the maps and radio bag into my map case and tucked my sweater in a corner of the seat. The sun helmet I'd better hold, I thought, while

we took off, in case it blew down on the floor
and got caught in the controls.

My husband, standing on the wing and working
through the open hatch, was stowing our last
bundles in the baggage compartment and strap-
ping them down.

"All right—will you help me with the bilge
pump?"

I climbed down again. The sterns of the pontoons were completely submerged. I had never
seen them so far down before. How would we
ever get at the rear compartments? I knelt on the
nose of first one pontoon and then the other, trying to tip the back portion up out of the water,
while my husband pumped.

"That's good—we're ready now—I'll take off the
anchor bridle."

I climbed back into the cockpit. We were all
ready and it was still dark—I looked at the horizon—but there were pink streaks in the sky and
you could see a little more of the surface of the
water. Not much wind—but it might come up at
sunrise. I switched on the light for a moment—
five-twenty—we could still get off before six. I
should try to contact Pan American—hour and
half hour. Better get the coils ready beforehand.

My husband took down the mooring light and
its pole (the mast of our rubber boat). He handed
the lantern and a canteen of kerosene to the men

in the boat. "Would you take these back to Government House for us? We can get some more on the other side." He jumped down onto the pontoons, cast loose the buoy rope and unhooked the bridle from the struts. "And this, too, we can replace this." He handed over the dripping coil of rope. "Good-by—" They shook hands in the dusk. "Good-by—" He climbed up into his cockpit and pulled on his helmet hurriedly. The plane drifted back very slowly from the buoy. "All clear?—Contact!" The whine of the self-starter. The first cold splutters of the engine, smoothing out into an even roar. The rush of wind. I clung to the helmet, wisps of hair whipping in my eyes. Now we had started—fasten the belt—cotton in the ears—watch—what time is it? Five-thirty. We could still be off before six.

The plane began to nose out toward the open bay, leaving the small cove, the docks and buoys behind, but so slowly and heavily, heaving from side to side as it pushed across waves in the current. It had never felt like this before. It actually seemed to creak, tired and lumbering, like a fat old woman puffing up stairs. Could this be our swift and powerful machine? I glanced over the wing. As my husband opened the throttle, the water rolled up still farther over the half-submerged pontoons. And when we rocked over a slightly bigger wave the wing-tips seemed to touch the water.

What a load we must have! Would we ever get off? There wasn't much wind, either. These waves here must be tide-rip; there were only small surface ripples from the wind. Farther out, I could see in the graying dawn, a darker band of water— larger waves—real wind, perhaps. We would take off against it. Toward the harbor entrance, then, the town on our left. There were still a few dim lights under the dark line of palms on the horizon. We were going at right angles, now, to our take-off direction. We would taxi over the stretch of water, searching it beforehand for native boats and bits of driftwood.

It took so long, this lumbering ride, the engine grinding ahead steadily, the plane rocking clumsily. The sky was much lighter. I looked at my watch. We had been ten minutes already. We turned down-wind, the plane wallowing in the tide-rip. Now, we were sweeping the take-off stretch. It was no longer rocky, but a slow steady drag like horses pulling through snow. There was enough light to see inside the cockpits. My husband reached back and set the master compass, on the floor between us, South-West, our course across the ocean to South America. The swinging arrow would be kept between those two white lines. The plane would stay on that course for thirteen hours—until we reached Fernando de Noronha.

He was turning. The wings teetered again. The plane was pointed to the harbor mouth. He pulled back the throttle, the engine idled, just ticking over. We were ready.

In the front cockpit, I saw my husband's head turn and, in the pause—while the engine idled, while the waves lapped the pontoons—heard his voice giving the familiar, "All set?"

I felt my safety belt to make sure it was closed and clung to the helmet in my hand. "All right." It had begun. I glanced at my watch and held my breath.

Blast of noise, rush of spray, storming over us, throbbing in our ears, streaming over the pontoons, the wings, the cockpits, pounding through the seats. Maelstrom of sound and spray, both inextricably mixed in a roar of power, covered us completely, enclosed us, cut us off from the world. No sound outside the engine's blast; no sight beyond the wall of spray. We were wrapped in the curl of a wave; we were poised in the heart of a typhoon. How could man keep his bearings in such a whirlwind? How could he control it, keep the plane steady, hold the reins taut? Somehow, he must. There was a central core of control, a balancing wheel. The plane was steady. It followed the lead of the rider, charging ahead through the water.

But this, I knew, was only the first stage, this blind charging through water like a creature of water. A few seconds only, one could stand that, then we would rise on top. A few seconds—I waited breathless for the spray to fall below, for the world to reappear, for the plane to emerge, spanking along on the top of the waves, "on the step." Now—now—trying to detect a difference in the sound, a change in that prolonged roar. There was no change. The long blast was still at the same pitch, the first deep breath of the engine. It had not yet found its second wind. Suspended roar of power; cavern of spray—without end.

Yes, the roar lessened; the spray fell. He was pulling back the throttle. We stopped charging ahead. The plane wavered a moment, uncertain, and then sank down abruptly, settled back in the water. No longer trying to climb, no longer fighting, engulfed again by the sea. A great backwash surged over the pontoons. With no motion, now, of its own, it floundered heavily in the irregular rhythm of the waves. The roar subsided to the steady whine of an engine idling. We could hear the waves lapping the pontoons; we could see the world around us. We were out in the middle of the bay. The sun was rising over the far shore, a liquid orange ball through the slight haze on the horizon. There were the quiet docks and ships behind us; there was the motionless line of palms and buildings on our left. We could not get off.

I looked at my watch—two minutes only—it had seemed hours. I started breathing regularly again. We could not get off. We could not even get "up on the step." What was it—no wind? Overload? Or both? Now, what would we do?

My husband opened the throttle. We tilted back slightly in the water. The plane started to turn, slowly, and heavily. Slowly and heavily we went back, over the long trail of white wake we had made, the engine chugging monotonously, the wings dipping from side to side. We were going to try again.

CHAPTER XXI

"IF WE HAD A WIND—"

W E'LL have to take out some fuel," my husband shouted from the cockpit. We were taxiing slowly back to the dock after our second unsuccessful attempt to get off the water. I looked at my watch. It was after six-thirty. How long would we be unloading? An hour anyway. These things always took forever. The hours spent working on the plane on the water seem interminable compared to the swift ones in the air. Could we still make the flight today? We would not get off until seven-thirty or eight, two hours later than we had planned. And with less fuel, we would have to cut down our speed in the air. We couldn't make Fernando de Noronha before dark—no, not possibly, I figured out. We would have to sacrifice that reserve of daylight. But we would have better moonlight for landing. We could still make it today if we didn't take too long unloading.

The plane pushed up gently to its old mooring buoy. The rowboat was still there with the two

Englishmen and the Negro guards who had stayed to see us off.

"What's the matter, Colonel?"

"Overload, that's all—have to take out some of the fuel. Have you got a pump there?"

We tied up to the buoy again and started to work on the plane.

"I'll take it out of the pontoon tanks," said my husband, unscrewing the cap. But the pump was too big to fit into the mouth of the tank. "Have you a smaller piece of hose? We can syphon it out." A smaller hose was found in the bottom of the boat. It fitted quite well but the fuel would not run out. "We'll have to suck on it to get it started." One of the Negro boys got down in the boat and put his mouth to the hose. Suck and spit, suck and spit—the fuel trickled out of the pipe and spread in shining rings over the surface of the water. "Doesn't seem to be coming very fast." My husband, kneeling on the pontoons, put the hose into his mouth. Suck and spit, suck and spit. "How about using the bilge pump? Get it out, will you—it's in the baggage compartment." I climbed over the fuselage and slid down onto the wing. "All right—here it is."

"Got another piece of hose? Look, we can cut this—" They fitted the hose to the bilge pump and started pumping. Finally—the even knock of the plunger, the rhythmic slosh of the gasoline—

we started unloading our fuel. Knock, knock, knock, it went on monotonously, the rhythm breaking only when the men took turns on the pontoon. I sat squatting on the spreader bar, holding the hose pressed down into the tank. An hour went by and we were still pumping. Seven-thirty. The sun felt pleasantly warm on my back. Men were moving about the docks, rolling barrels into warehouses, stretching nets along the ground. Through the gates I could see natives padding by with baskets on their heads. Cars blew their horns in the distance and carts creaked and rumbled as they went past on their way to town. The day had started, people were already about, getting on with their work. And we were still pumping fuel out of our tanks. Our head start on the rest of the world, I thought—desperately, where was it going to?

"There—that's enough now," said my husband. "But I think we had better pump out the pontoons again—there may be some water in those back compartments."

He opened the anchor box. It was full of water. We pumped it dry. "Those back compartments, now—" They were still submerged in spite of the lightened load. "Do you think we could move the rowboat around there in back, and get one of the boys to lift up on the tail?" The Negro boys, giggling and shouting, shouldered the tail, like Atlas.

The tops of the pontoons just cleared the water line. We unscrewed the caps and started to pump. The water sloshed out into the bay, foaming and dirty. Another hour went by. Boats were moving about. Shadows were no longer crisp and sharp on land. We squinted to avoid the blaze of sun on the water. Eight-thirty—about the time we would have breakfasted at Government House. Our head start had completely gone. How long it took!

Finally we were ready. We handed over our things. We said good-by again, and started out into the bright bay. The ship was definitely lighter—all that fuel out. It really ought to help. We didn't flounder about so badly either. Much better. Or was the bay calmer? The water stretched an even muddy color ahead of us. There were no darker patches to show a breeze-ruffled surface. There was not a sign of a whitecap, even out toward the harbor mouth. Still, we were not so heavy; we might get off.

We trailed down the long stretch of water and turned again. I looked at my watch—almost nine —what a late start. "All set?" "Yes—all right." We started again. The roar—the spray— This time we emerged. The spray fell behind. We were up on the step, spanking along on the surface, still water-bound, but no longer blindly enclosed, half a creature of water and half of air. Spank, spank,

spank. This was only the second stage. These spanks should quicken, faster, faster, until suddenly they ceased altogether and the plane, no longer fighting, had cleared even the tips of the waves—had reached the air, its own element, where it had no rivals, no opposition, and the engine could breathe easily in a sigh of triumph.

Spank, spank—there was no quickening of the rhythm. There was no lift into the air. Spank, spank, spank—they didn't stop. They would go on and on as long as we drove relentlessly across the broad bay. That miraculous moment when the vibrations ironed out into a smooth climb would never come. A bird with clipped wings, we couldn't get off.

"The wind has died," said my husband, "that's the trouble." We taxied back to dock. The boat was still sitting by the buoy. It was beginning to be very hot. The Englishmen had on their sun helmets. They looked up, waiting for us to speak.

"Can't quite make it," my husband said. "It's much better—gets up on the step all right, but can't quite get off—if we had a little wind I think we could do it." He looked back at the bay.

The men followed his glance across the muddy ripples. "There's no wind at all right now—it's died down completely," they agreed, pulling up to the pontoons.

"Well," said my husband, jumping down out

of the cockpit, "there's no use trying any more now." He reached for the bridle.

"When do you think you will try again, Colonel?"

"It just depends on the wind. If we had a wind we would take off this afternoon—" He snapped down the bridle fasteners.

"You won't get any breeze this afternoon, I'm afraid"—one of the Englishmen shook his head doubtfully—"there never is any."

"Tonight, then," said my husband, tightening the ropes. "There isn't anything else to do—we can't take off glass water with our load. We'll just have to wait for a wind."

What good was it trying to plan ahead? Daybreak—dusk, moonrise—moonset, light—darkness: all these factors sank to secondary importance, subject to that one vital element over which we had no control—wind. That was the keystone of the puzzle, the masterpiece. We would have to wait for the wind.

CHAPTER XXII

"THE SUN AND STARS ARE MINE"

W E drove back to Government House with our bundles. The streets were now full of people; bright calicos and swinging skirts, turbaned heads and straw hats, bobbing along the sidewalks; the ping of bicycle bells, the shuffle and slap of bare feet on pavement, and the constant indistinct sing-song of voices; the hot smell of dust and animal, of food cooking somewhere, of chickens in baskets on their way to market. The morning was in full swing. Everyone was busy; only we were not. For us the day yawned bright and empty, a day we should not have had. We should have been in the air, alone, far from Bathurst, far on our way across the ocean toward Natal.

What would we do with this extra unwanted day? The cessation of work, the easing of tension, left us slack and limp. For we were no longer fighting against anything, not against time, or the growing light, or the waves, or the weight of the plane.

We climbed the steps of Government House,

171

feeling like ghosts. (It can't be us—we were not to be here today. Today we were flying across the Atlantic.)

The Governor and his wife had breakfast waiting for us. "Well—what happened? You couldn't get off? Wasn't the wind right?"

We started to tell our story. "Yes—at first—but our load was too heavy . . ." We went over our long struggle down the bay. "—and then we unloaded our fuel . . ." They listened sympathetically. "—but by that time the wind had died."

"What hard luck—so now . . . ?"

"So now we are waiting for a wind. We'll take off with the first one we get."

It did not seem so difficult when we talked about it. Your own problems never seem difficult looked at through the eyes of outsiders. They listen only to your words and base their conclusions on them alone. But your own conclusions are only half based on what you say and at least half on unspoken facts—on elements surrounding the problem which are sometimes, perhaps, unknown and unperceived even by you, but nevertheless influence you.

After all, I thought, half convincing myself that our difficulties were over, it had been hard luck. The wind had died just as we got our load lightened. But now we were all ready to start, we should have no more trouble.

"Tonight, perhaps, or tomorrow morning, surely, you'll get a wind?"

"Oh, yes, we will—we'll just have to wait for it, that's all."

We finished our breakfast and took a nap. If we were going to fly tonight we would need the sleep. We forgot the long day we had already lived through, and started a new one. Tonight or tomorrow we would fly across the Atlantic.

In the late afternoon ("There's no wind in the harbor?" "No—no wind.") we went out to "Cape House" on a promontory overlooking the sea. We drove through gardens dripping with shade and tangled flowering vines, purple Bougainvillea, yellow Allamanda. We swam in a pool and sat, rested, on a terrace, looking over the water. Tea in thermos bottles, cushions to sit on, and the darkening world at our feet.

The cliff below us fell abruptly to the sea. The sea poured out, a great wide circle, to the sky. No bumps on the horizon, no islands broke that smooth expanse, rolled out like heavy corded silk to the edge of the world. Only one point of land down the coast—the plumed head of a palm, the jagged outline of a rock—reached out like a last articulately formed word against the great dark speechless stretch of ocean.

The sky was clear and limpid like some amber

fluid, no wisps of cloud, no shreds of mist. The
sun sank, a single globule of gold, through depths
of liquid sky into a liquid sea. There were no
dregs of day left behind, no untidy streaks of
color, no blur of afterglow. It had been day; now
it was night. Eyes, filled brimful of bright sky,
turned to the land, startled to find it was dark;
turned to the sea, surprised to find the waves, like
the nap of velvet, brushed dark with a single
stroke; turned to the sky again, to find pale silver
pinpricks in its satin surface.

So imperceptibly night came, so peacefully.
Here there was no struggle. Earth, sea, and sky—
we had been in them this morning, fighting
against them. Why, I wondered? Now, looking
down on them, it seemed incredible—now they
were spread out in all their calm beauty below
us.

The waves, no longer our opponents, on the
rocks below, beat out an even rhythm, soothing
to our ears. The sky, neither light nor dark, to
be hoarded or spent, was only beautiful to our
eyes. Nature was no longer the unjust opponent.
She swept her gifts equally, on us sitting here on
the terrace; on a boat, not visible before, now
showing a tiny prick of light on the horizon; on
that last point of land pushing out to sea; on the
harbor around the corner at Bathurst. Beauty of

earth and sky and water was here for us to take, lying peacefully at our feet.

> The Earth, the Seas, the Light, the lofty Skies,
> The Sun and Stars are mine; if these I prize.[1]

For gradually we were looking not at earth and sea but up at the stars. The pendulum of the mind swings first over land; then, wider, over the sea; and finally stretches to take in its compass the sky. Arcturus, Aldebaran, Alpheratz—the names sang in my mind like a half-remembered line of a poem. But I did not see any stars that I knew. I was not looking for navigating stars, only those bright points of light that shake out of the corners before the sky is fully clothed. Pale, at first, and shy—they disappear when you look right at them—gradually they bloom out of the dark; they dwarf the dark. They, and not the dark, are the sky. And, as you stare, they fasten upon you, draw you upward, until you feel no longer rooted in the earth. Arcturus, Aldebaran, Alpheratz—if only you could have your point of balance the sky! With such a pivot you could hold the world on your shoulders, another Atlas. In such an armor you could meet anything.

I turned and faced the dark sea. Suddenly I was aware that the feeling of cool strength flowing over me—against my face, past my ears,

---

[1] Thomas Traherne, "The Salutation."

through my hair—was wind. And in the vast pattern of earth and sky and water, I was conscious only of that one element—wind. Like a familiar voice speaking to you through a light sleep, the wind roused us, and we woke, startled, shook off our dreams, stiffened to an old role. We put on our armor, half asleep still, but spurred to action.

"Look—there's a wind—a strong wind!"

We jumped up and leaned over the parapet.

"Can you see—down there—I think there are whitecaps—"

"Yes," said my husband. His words clipped out like heels on a stone pavement hurrying somewhere. "Yes—we'll leave at midnight."

CHAPTER XXIII

"WITH A MOON—"

ALL set? We're about ready." My husband was untying the mooring lantern from the engine cowling.

"Yes, all right." I half turned in my cockpit and stretched out my arm so that the light fell on my wristwatch. Eleven-thirty—we were down on the bay again, in our plane, still tied up to the buoy, but ready to take off at midnight.

The events of the last hours, since we left the terrace on the cape, had fallen one after another in quick succession, machine-like and precise, like the cycle of an engine. No delay, no hesitation, not one out of time, all driving ahead with the force of our excitement behind them. "There's a wind—we'll take off at midnight."

Back to Government House. Out to the pier. No time to watch the fish tonight. "Flounder, flounder"—is there a wind? Yes—a good wind, even here in the harbor. Roll up our bundles. Last messages to Pan American. Supper— "Good-by, good-by, you're coming to see us off? At midnight, yes." Down to the bay at nine-thirty. Pack up the plane. Pump out the pontoons. Yes—a good wind; I even need my sweater on. There's the moon.

All our actions since tea-time seemed to have been crowded into a few minutes, telescoped by some outside pressure. My emotions too, those tremendous ones that leaped like giants at the words "take off at midnight"—those too were all under pressure, squeezed into a tiny space, pushed down, coil on coil, and the lid fastened down tight like a jack-in-the-box. Mustn't let them out. No time, no space. Hold them in until after the take-off. Then there would be plenty of time, sixteen hours of flying and nothing else; plenty of space, eighteen hundred miles of empty ocean. For we were taking off at midnight across the Atlantic.

Now that we were down in the plane again, equipped, packed up, ready to go, the day in between telescoped, too, into nothing. We were back in the struggle, taking off, like this morning. Only now it was night; it was dark.

It had been dark this morning, too, but a shallow and impermanent darkness, a receding tide. We had been working all the time toward light. Temporary blindness we could put up with, for each second brought us nearer to sight. Still swimming over our depth in night, each stroke brought us nearer day. But tonight, it was different. We were sunk in night, fathoms deep. There was no reaching out. We must work in it and with it. We must come to terms with the dark.

There was a moon, of course, only one night past full. But even with a moon, I thought, suddenly feeling a stranger to the world, how little one saw, compared to day. There was light enough for walking down the road. You would not bump into anything. Even small stones showed up, frosted with moonlight, under your feet. But they were close to you. Once you started to look at things a little farther away, your vision faded with frightening rapidity. Looking back at the shore line from the water, you could see only the surrounding harbor, and that dimly; the outlines of trees against the sky, but not their texture, not their distance from one another; the shadowy black of the pier stretching out into the blacker water, but not its substance, not its depth. The world was lit, but badly. It would do for a slow pace only, a man walking, or at most, the trot of a horse. But not for the speed of a plane, where all ill-defined objects would merge into one blur of shadow as you went by. There was no precision to a moonlit world. At best, you could only fumble. And you must not fumble in flying.

Working on the plane was not difficult. The general outlines of fuselage, wings, and pontoons, when you were next to them, showed almost as

clearly as by day. At times you forgot it was night.
But even here, working on details, you felt blind.
We needed a flashlight to pump out the pontoons,
to see just what angle to put in the hose, to replace the cap. If we needed light for a little thing
like that, I thought, how could my husband see
to take off? How could he see boats and buoys
and driftwood in our path? How could he judge
waves and wind, the angle of the plane, the distance off the water, and a thousand other vital
factors that must depend on sight?

The street lamps were not much help. When
you were near, they lit up very well the small
circle around them, a gate, a corner of a shed, a
ladder. But farther away, they were only lamps
and lit nothing. They were only signposts to say:
here is a corner, here is a road, here is a dock.
There the lights trembled and flattened out in
elongated crimped ribbons. Those were reflec-
tions and not lights at all. That was water, then.
But where did water begin and land end? There
was no clear line of demarcation.

Where did land meet sky? Looking up, I could
see the dark indistinct masses of trees and house
tops against a less dark sky. And then the stars
began. There was no mistaking sky. You could
see the horizon indisputably, but not sharply. No
details were sharp anywhere, except those silver
ripples cut out metallically in the bright path of

the moon. How could we take off in such a strange world?

Here inside the cockpit it was less strange. I could feel my way. Everything in its place? The radio key—the earphones—the drift indicator—the transmitter and receiver boxes. I touched them all for comfort, not that anything could have moved, but to assure myself of a familiar world. I would put away my things. I would get ready my papers—the regular routine—write down the form of the first message.

We would be started soon, now. He had untied the lantern and handed it down to the boat. Now, even that faint glow which had thrown a small shining circle on the black cowling—even that was out. We had no artificial light. Was there one in the front cockpit? I leaned forward around the seat which blocked my vision. The luminous dials of the instrument board, silvered numbers and hands, stood out of the blackness like disembodied spirits, suspended in the cockpit. These he could fly by, of course; these were his eyes. I had forgotten them.

The wing-lights flicked on; red on the left wing-tip, green on the right—match-flares in the night. The engine started with a blast, the sound of it reassuringly the same in a strange world of sight. We turned slowly, the lights of the shore swinging behind us as we faced the dark bay.

Looking back, the shadowy masses of boats and docks, houses and trees, all blended into one shadow that was land; a dark band indiscriminately dotted with lights, a stretch of starred land between the thinly starred sky and the black starless water.

Ahead, the moon lay bright on the water, a deceptive brightness which gave light but not much vision. We were heading into it. Soon we turned, the lights on the wing-tips dipping as we crossed the waves. We were going down-wind to sweep our take-off stretch. The town was at our right hand, the harbor mouth behind us, the moon at our backs. The water, the horizon line, the tops of the trees against the sky, were flooded with a dim mist of light, whose source was uncertain. We plowed ahead into its strange brightness. But we were not taking off in this direction. We would have to take off toward the wind, toward the harbor entrance, almost toward the moon.

I heard the engine climb and the answering rush of pontoons through the water. My husband had opened up the throttle. He was checking the instruments, those bright numbers in the dark. We must be almost ready to turn. Another blast of the engine. We were at the end of the stretch, starting to turn. The plane lurched—ease back the throttle—give her her head—yes, she was swinging —slowly, clumsily, but unerringly into the wind.

CHAPTER XXIV

"IF WE TAKE OFF AT NIGHT—"

WE were ready to start. I could see where we were, now. How far out we had gone. That thin line of lights on our left was the town. That thin band of dark on our right showed the opposite shore. Ahead, where the line blotted out indistinctly, that must be the harbor entrance. And here was the moon, full and high and brilliant, not quite facing us, coming in at an angle on our right, striking in its sparkling path the opposite shore, the waves in the bay, the gleaming curve of the wing, the shining cockpit covers, our faces. One narrow strip of vision in a dim world, one peephole in the night—this was what we were counting on. We must take off by this alone. We were not riding down that bright path, but we must use it, as a person in a dark room at night builds up out of the blackness, the walls, the doors, the chairs and tables, all from one slit of light through the shutters. How much that moonlit strip must tell to the pilot—waves and wind, direction and speed, height and balance.

He must plunge ahead into the darkness,

guided by that silver ribbon in his right hand. We had flown like that before, I remembered, never taking off the water by moonlight, but through bad weather by day. Sometimes we had to push through the edge of a storm, blind in front of us, with only a small strip of sun-flecked field shining on our right, ahead, under the skirts of the rain. Green—hold on to that piece of green, I would think; that will pull us through. It took such faith to fly, I thought then, when the rain beat black on the wind-shield—to fly only by a small piece of green in your right hand. It was like walking through a dark passage as a child, your eyes on the light shining in the room beyond. But this—this was worse still, tonight. This *was* the dark passage and we must go ahead with only a hand brushing the side of the wall.

The dark—the dark—all childish terror of the dark poured back over me. What was there in the dark out there? How could he see? How could he control the plane? We would hook a wing into the water. We would be thrown, caught, drowned —that plane off Portugal— If only it were not dark —just for a second—if only—

"All set?"

"Yes, all right."

The noise, the spray, the dark; we were wrapped in all three tonight, spun in a cocoon, layer on layer about us. One could see nothing—

nothing. No, but he could feel, I had forgotten that. I could feel, too, that gigantic lift the plane made against the wall of water. The rush—the climb. Tense, I held my breath. This time we'll get off. Watch the wing-tip—on fire! No—only the flow of spray past the red light. How can he see—anything—even the path of the moon? No, but above? The stars—the stars were clear above. Out of this welter below they were fixed. They were unchanged. He could steer by the stars, pivot on them—Arcturus, Aldebaran.

There—we were out of the spray. She's up on the step, spanking along, driving across the bay, swift and straight as a bullet. And there was the moon, the bright path of the moon, ahead of us, racing along at our side, keeping pace with us, lighting our road like some friendly power, some swift goddess, always ahead. For we would not outstrip that path, no more than one could as a child, racing the moon in a train. No matter how fast one rushed—through towns and fields, tunnels and bridges, charging ahead at full speed—at each little pond, each bend of river, each sliver of marsh, the moon was there first. We would not outrun the moon. A goddess—no, perhaps, a will-of-the-wisp—it would run before us, leading us on and on across the bay, out of the harbor, into the sea even, if we followed it. But surely—

The sound changed. The roar slackened. He

pulled back the throttle. The plane balked, hesitated a second, sank back into the sea. Down from the silver path, out of the swift track, into the trough of the waves. The water washed up around us, heaving us this way and that. The plane floundered uncertainly. The engine whined. We couldn't make it, then.

But why, why? What was the matter? I sat, still clasping my radio bag tightly in the back seat. What was wrong? We had a good wind—more than any time before. I even had my sweater on. We got up on the step, too. The moon was with us. Why couldn't we get off? If only he would tell me, something, anything. But I mustn't ask. We were still in the middle of it. Never ask anything in the middle of it. Upsetting. He's got enough to think about. But if he would only look around, I could see; I could tell perhaps, by the side of his face.

He did not look around; he was looking straight ahead. He was turning the plane, slowly and heavily wallowing in the waves. The moon slid behind us; the lights reappeared. We were going back. We would try again.

The plane commenced its long trek back over the water. I relaxed and started breathing regularly. I began to feel sick from excitement. I didn't want to be sick. It was absurd, I argued. Look at the stars. Remember this evening, the

Cape. The stars—calm, peace. Remember you thought human misery small; human life unimportant. Arcturus, Aldebaran, Alpheratz—keep me from my fear. Arcturus, Aldebaran, Alpheratz —those were only words. Concentrate on the stars. Try to name them. That big circle there—the navigating stars—Capella, Castor, Pollux. Was that the Southern Cross? What did it point to? Think now, what did it point to—couldn't remember. The plane bobbed up and down. I felt sick.

He was turning now. He was going to try again. Get out your watch. Time it. By moonlight? Yes—I could see. The moon must be higher. Or my eyes accustomed to the dark, now, seeing more, cat's eyes.

"All set?"

"Yes, all right."

This time just look at your watch. Don't think —count—one—two—three—four . . . forty-five— forty-six—forty-seven—forty-eight. Spank—spank— spank—spank.

No—no use. He was pulling back the throttle. We sank back into the water. What was the matter? Oh—what *was* the matter? He turned the plane again, slowly, heavily. Why didn't he tell me something? He cut the switch. The engine kicked out a few last protesting sputters. It was suddenly still and peaceful. The lights twinkled in the distance from the shore. The stars shone unmoved over our heads. The moonlight fell gently over our shoulders into the cockpit. We were two people alone, bobbing about in the chop in the middle of the bay at night.

There was a long silence, only the waves slapping on the pontoons, only the wind against our ears, only the creak of the plane rocking from side to side.

Finally, I spoke. "What are you going to do?" My voice sounded flat and ordinary out of the stillness.

"Don't know—thought we'd think about it." He was discouraged. "It almost gets off—almost. I don't understand it."

The fire had gone out of his words but he still hoped we could get off.

What should I say? How should I try to swing things? Should I say what I really felt, "Let's not take any more chances—go back to bed?" No—that was just weakness—mustn't give in to it. Besides, it was silly, I knew he didn't take chances. Should I force myself to say, "Come, let's try again?" No, I didn't know enough about it—better leave it to him. I said nothing.

The plane bobbed up and down; the waves slapped against the pontoons. I waited, sitting still, hanging on to my radio bag in the dark.

"Well," the voice from the front cockpit, "I

think we'd better go back and get a good night's rest and think things over."

"Oh—" Relief—warm relief and tiredness flooded through me. But don't say anything. Don't give in to it, not yet.

The head in the front cockpit turned. "We'll try again on the way home."

"On the way home," I thought. That shows how little hope he has. I tried to key myself up to another take-off. It was no use. I could not get back to that level. We could not get off. The evening had gone flat. The terror and the beauty, both, had vanished. The stars were not pivots for our flight. The wind was not a voice calling us to action. The plane was not a bullet, but only a clumsy water-bound boat. The moon was not a goddess, racing us, guiding us on. It was only the moon—and it was waning.

CHAPTER XXV

EARTH-BOUND

WE turned toward the narrow strip of lights and taxied slowly back. We couldn't get off. I tried to think what it meant. We had a wind, we had lightened the plane—and we couldn't get off. We had taken off with a load as heavy as that before, too, in Greenland. Why couldn't we get off now?

The shore loomed up, dark against the sky, light against the water as we pushed nearer.

What was the matter—what more could we do? I argued with myself. We couldn't leave behind any more fuel. We were down to the limit without taking chances. Would we wait and wait for a really strong wind? But was there ever a strong wind at Bathurst? And the moon was waning every night. Would we wait here a month for another moon? Would we tear every unnecessary thing out of the plane, the floorboards, our baggage, and try again? Would we move to another place? Dakar was out of the question, of course. But there was Portuguese Guinea. There was Liberia. What else was there on the coast of

190

Africa? But then—sickening question at the bottom of my mind—could we get off at all with enough load to make it?

All those questions, I could not ask my husband. For one thing he did not have the answers himself, I suspected. And it would be unfair to ask for them, to throw the scorching light of my curiosity upon them when they were still underground. They would grow, I knew, but slowly and in the dark, the answers to those unasked questions. And I must wait, and not force them, or they would wither, pale shoots that could not stand the light of day.

Besides, we were too tired tonight, overwhelmingly weary and depressed. Would we have felt like this if we had got off? Was it the weight of the day's work on our shoulders or simply the weight of failure, that made us feel heavy and earth-bound, like our overloaded plane? One question would have been too much. The merest word, the lightest feather of a doubt, would have been more than one could carry, I felt, and would put one right under the waters of despair.

The engine whirred ahead in the night; the pontoons nosed on through the water. We were coming in to the small cove. The outlines on shore began to distinguish themselves. Docks pushed out from the shadows. Houses squared off against the sky. Masts lined up here and there in the dim mist of moonlight. Lights twinkled on familiar corners; the road, the pier, the buoy, the little rowboat with a flickering lantern. It was all dishearteningly the same. And we too, pushing back to port as we had done before. Nothing had happened. We couldn't get off.

The guards were still there; I never expected to see them again. There was even someone on the dock. I could see the outline of standing figures. I hoped it was not the Governor and his wife. I couldn't bear to see them again tonight, to face their kindness.

My husband cut the switch. In the dead stillness that followed we drifted up to the buoy. What a lifeless night it was! Here in the cove, the wind, the noise, all motion had died. My husband climbed down on the pontoon and reached for the bridle, without saying anything. He made fast to the buoy, and lashed the pole and lantern to the cowling. I pulled out the bundles from our baggage compartment and handed them down to the boys without a word. We closed up the cockpit covers. We stepped into the boat and sat down in the back, hugging our bundles on our laps. In silence we creaked back to shore.

There was one Englishman on the pier who had stayed to see us in. He pulled up our bundles without saying anything and helped us up the ladder.

"What's the matter now, Colonel?" he said kindly, as we picked up our things and stood with our backs to the bay. His voice was patient and gentle like your grandmother's when you got a knot in your sewing. Just as casual, too, and as taken for granted—"Back again, Anne dear, what is the matter now—another knot?"

"Don't know—overload, that's all," said my husband with some appearance of cheerfulness. "We've taken off with that much before." (He's worried about that, too, then.) "It must be different down here in the tropics—maybe the density of the air."

"Hmm—it's been very damp today," said the Englishman mildly.

The Governor's car was waiting at the gate. We walked along the pier, our footsteps clicking in the silence, our blurred shadows slanting ahead in the moonlight.

The car door slammed sharply in the night. The engine purred.

"Well, we thought we'd sleep on it," said my husband, leaning forward to say good night.

"Oh, yes, always wise, always wise—" said the Englishman, as he stepped back under the street lamp. "Good night."

It was after one. We drove home in complete silence, looking straight ahead of us, I still clasping the radio bag on my lap. There was no one in the streets. The accelerator rose and sank gustily as we gained speed on the open stretches and slowed up at the corners. A few huddled forms were asleep on the stone benches near the market place. The town was dead.

We stole quietly into Government House. No one was awake, thank goodness. Up the stairs with our bundles. Into our room. Our pile of discarded equipment faced us blankly as we opened the door.

"It's better not to get too tired," said my husband at last. "Then you begin taking chances—a great many accidents happen that way."

I was relieved to have him speak, even if his mouth was set. ("There's nothing to do but soldier," I remember he said sometimes.) It meant things were not so bad.

"We've still got a few tricks we can pull," he said with a smile.

We'll fool them yet, I thought, inconsequently, my spirits rising to his remark. Who "they" were, I did not know—the harbor at Bathurst, the load, the damp, the wind, or the Englishman at the dock.

But I did not ask about the "tricks." We went to bed without talking at all and pulled the dark, the comforting dark, up over our heads.

CHAPTER XXVI

A FEW TRICKS

WHEN we finally woke the next morning, heavy, weary, drugged with sleep and confused memories, there was a stack of cablegrams on the breakfast table, waiting for us. Apparently, we had not been "two people alone out in the middle of the bay." Apparently, a great many other people had been there too, and, even if we did not, they knew what was wrong and wished to advise us. Some of the messages were attempting to be helpful and some were just amusing, but all of them were rather hazy about the facts.

"I suppose they've been reading the newspapers again," I said, ruefully, as we slit them open.

"They have certainly got the propeller company excited," said my husband. "Read this: 'PRESS REPORTS YOU USING WOOD PROPELLER'—Where did they get that idea?—'PLEASE CABLE WHY METAL PROPELLER UNSATISFACTORY.'"

"Yes," said someone at the table, "there was a report saying that Colonel Lindbergh was seen filing the splinters off his wood propeller."

"Splinters!" I exclaimed. "What do they think we're flying, a Jenny?"

"Here's one from the pontoon people—'SUG-GEST BARNACLE INSPECTION.'" I looked up, astonished. "Do you think there are any *barnacles* on the pontoons?"

"Don't think so," said my husband. "The plane hasn't been in tropical water long enough. You do get them, though, on seaplanes down here."

"Barnacles," I said—"even barnacles; there's no end to what one must contend with in flying."

"The engine company has sent us a wire, too," went on my husband. "They think we should postpone the trip till they test this type of engine a little more. They think something may be wrong with it—"

"*Do* they?" I said sarcastically. "This is a fine time to discover that—"

"Well," said my husband, his optimism restored, "we are not going to postpone it. The engine is all right. So are the pontoons and so is the propeller. And we have a lot of things up our sleeve yet."

"You haven't another moon, have you—or a strong wind?"

"No," he smiled, "no—but we can lighten our load a great deal still."

"How? You can't take out any more fuel."

"Not gas, no," he said, "but we've more oil

than we need. It's rather a job to take out. That's why I didn't bother to before—hardly seemed worth while—but now, every pound counts, every ounce."

"Yes, of course. Our clothes, for instance—that's eighteen pounds apiece," I figured out, "we can leave them behind. And the camera and films— they are not heavy though. It's too bad to—"

"Yes—but they're not necessary. We can't afford to take anything we don't need. There's another bag of emergency food I can get out—butter and chocolate rations we had for the ice-cap—stored in the tail. It was out of the way back there and helped to balance the plane. Hard to get at—means taking the seat out, but we can save quite a lot there."

"Anything else?"

"Well, there's the empty gas tank we are not using, ahead of the baggage compartment—all un-necessary weight. I can get in there and snip that out. There are other things, too," he went on, "lightening the tool kit, for instance. Leave the engine crank behind—you'd be surprised how much weight we can save." He got up to leave for the harbor.

"It's very interesting," he said, turning back at the door with a smile—"very interesting, all this experience."

It was stiflingly hot in the harbor at Bathurst, although the noonday heat was over. Shadows of masts and docks were lengthening slowly across the blinding water. It was already mid-afternoon. But the red lacquer wings and the fuselage of the plane remained scorched from the rays of the sun. My husband was still working in the airless hole of the baggage compartment, cutting out piece by piece, with a huge pair of tin-snips, the unused gasoline tank.

Everything else was done. He had taken out the back seat and crawled into the tail to get at the extra bag of emergency food. He had drained the oil. He had collected in the rowboat a small heap of extra equipment, to be added to the pile in our bedroom. One of the Negro boys had wiped the hulls of the pontoons, lying down on his stomach on top and reaching underneath with his arm. (They would not go into the water for fear of sharks.) There were no barnacles but there was always a certain amount of deposit. If this roughness were rubbed off, it might reduce the friction slightly.

Now there was only the gas tank. It couldn't be pulled out, embodied as it was in the oval fuselage. And it was not a question of simply cutting out a great hollow container. The tank was honey-combed with partitions to keep the gasoline from sloshing about unevenly, and had to be torn out piece by piece. My husband crouched down in the compartment and worked the huge tin-snips with both arms, throwing out from time to time, through the open hatch, jagged scraps of duralumin. They fell lightly into the water and fluttered leaf-like to the bottom of the bay, the sun flashing on their bright sides as they went down.

It was one of those long jobs that could not be hurried and in which one could hardly notice any progress. One worked ahead slowly, like a worm gnawing through wood, and gradually it wore down the afternoon.

But as the day progressed, it became increasingly difficult to work. As soon as the tank was opened, the small slops of gasoline, still left in the bottom, began to vaporize. The fumes filled the compartment, the cockpit, my husband's lungs and eyes. By mid-afternoon, with the sun beating down on the thin shell of the plane, the atmosphere became almost unbearable. He worked in it as long as he could, then crawled out into the broiling sun for a breath of air. Clapping his helmet on his head, he stood in his soaked shirtsleeves on the burning wing. A Negro blacksmith, shining with perspiration, took his turn at the tank. When he could stand it no longer, my husband changed places with him again. Tea-time came and went. The sun reddened above the mangrove shores. And the small strips of silver metal still flicked down brightly into the bay of Bathurst.

It was almost supper-time when my husband came back to Government House.

"You look awfully tired," I said as he came into the room, his arms loaded with equipment.

"Yes," he answered, "I've been working inside the fuselage—the fumes were awful—gave me a headache. I've saved a lot of weight though—over two hundred pounds, I think."

He set his bundles on the floor and looked up with an air of triumph. "The tank must have weighed about a hundred pounds, and the oil another thirty. Then this sack of food"—he lifted it up and set it over against the old pile of equipment—"that must be thirty or thirty-five pounds."

"How marvelous!"

"Then nearly ten pounds of tools," he went on, adding up in his mind. "I've taken out almost everything except a few wrenches, a pair of pliers, and a screw driver."

"What's that—the sleeping bag?" I asked.

"Yes, that would only get wet on the ocean. We've still got our woolen clothing." He put the rest of the things on the pile; the engine crank, a funnel, another can of tetraethyl lead, the tools, and some ammunition.

"Gracious—what's left in the plane?"

"All our emergency equipment for a forced landing at sea," said my husband firmly, "I haven't taken out a single item. I've had to take out some of the land equipment, but that's not so vital— we've still got a gun and our first-aid kit."

"Well—here are our clothes and the camera and some radio pamphlets I've saved you. Are we all set to go tonight, then?"

"Yes, we're all set, but—let's walk down to the pier."

The Negro guards were padding softly by the gates of Government House. The palms stood up black in the airless sky. On the pier it was cool, although the bay was calm. No ripple broke that enigmatic surface. I looked under the light by the steps for some flicker in the water below. ("Flounder, Flounder in the sea—Prithee hearken unto me—") No silver fin appeared. Tonight there was no one to answer my questions.

My husband turned to let any coolness, any breath of air there might be, fall against his hot face. "I think," he said finally, "we had better get a good night's rest and try again tomorrow."

"I think," I answered without a moment's hesitation, "that's a very good idea."

The moon was waning; there would be less light tomorrow night. We might even miss a good wind this evening. It didn't matter. There was

something more important than either of these
factors. There was something else which was
equal to extra gasoline, a strong wind, less load,
better weather. It was something intangible, which
could not be weighed or measured, but I knew
that a night's sleep would give it to us.

CHAPTER XXVII

"LISTEN! THE WIND IS RISING"

> Listen! the wind is rising,
> and the air is wild with leaves—

I WAS lying on my bed in Government House, in the middle of the afternoon, learning poetry. There was nothing else to do. Everything was done. My husband was asleep. The plane was in shape. We were packed up, ready to go. And I was resting. We needed the rest for we were going to try again tonight, our last attempt to fly to South America from Bathurst.

"Could we take off tomorrow night?" I had asked my husband in the morning.

"Yes," he had said, doubtfully, "but that's about the last."

"Well, you could still take off at daybreak, couldn't you?" I had pursued.

"No—you see the moon rises later every night. There wouldn't be any moon at all when we reached South America."

I hesitated—that last question, "Could you get off now with *no* wind?"

"Almost!" he had said.

It was tonight, then, or—well, better not think about it. Rest; sleep; learn poetry. I opened my pocket scrapbook.

> Listen! the wind is rising,
>   and the air is wild with leaves . . .

I had copied those lines as we left England, in October; when the last of the dahlias hung clumsy golden heads above their blackened stalks; when leaves rose in gusty flames into the sky, lifting a whole tree before your eyes, bodily, it seemed, into the air. Elm and oak and beech—to think of them here gave me some of the peace of England.

> we have had our summer evenings—

(Like long English meadows, rolling out to the sky. There was strength in having them behind your back.)

> now for October eves!

It might help, too. Poetry did, sometimes, filling up the mind. I might need it tonight, bobbing up and down under the stars, or even plunging ahead through the dark sky, over the dark ocean—if we got off—

The great beech-trees lean forward,
    and strip like a diver—

(Bright copper leaves, turned up this way and that, burning like coals, under foot.)

    and strip like a diver. We—

That was enough, really. The rest was not for us.

    . . . We
    had better turn to the fire,
    and shut our minds to the sea—

We couldn't do that—not yet, anyway. We still had work to do.

    where the ships of youth are running
    close-hauled on the edge of the wind—

Oh—if only we had a wind like that! A wind you could bite into, a wind you could pull hard against, as you could in a boat, heeled over, the sail taut, bowed to the water; the tiller hard against your aching arm; your feet braced on the leeward seat; your cheeks in the wind, warm and tingling underneath but firm and chilled on the surface—like fruit. And the sound of water, rushing, gurgling, racing, tearing under you.

    where the ships of youth are running
    close-hauled on the edge of the wind,
    with all adventure before them . . .[1]

[1] Humbert Wolfe, "Autumn Resignation."

Yes, but that was the Maine coast I was thinking of. And this was Africa. There was the mosquito net over my head. Here was the white airless room. It was time for tea. And after tea, a drive to the Cape, and after that, supper, and after that—

Listen! the wind is rising—

I got up and dressed. I had tea. My husband went down to the bay.

"Is there anything to do?" I asked.

"No," he said. "But I think I'll just go down and look over the plane."

I knew how he felt—anything to fill up the afternoon.

The Governor's wife was taking me for a drive to the gardens where we were the other night. (There, at least, there will be a wind!) We got out and walked in the dusty shade of trees. ("The great beech-trees lean forward—") But these were not beech. They were Casuarina, with long whip-like branches spraying above our heads. They were spiny palm and strange gray-leaved trees whose name I did not know. The dry turf crackled under our feet. Spikes of cactus speared the sunshine. There was not a breath of wind, even here The tangled creepers dripped their yellow flowers, motionless in the still air. Insects rasped out their songs like sawdust. And small metallic-colored birds flicked brightly from one shrub of oleander to another, the only sign of life in that lifeless garden.

I could hardly look at the birds, at the lancet-leaved oleanders, at the trees, strangled with ropes of vine. Like someone in love, all sights, all objects, led back to one thing in my mind. As one might say, "But he is not here to see them," I could only think, "But there is no wind, even here." I could only see that the vines hung listless from their branches. There was not a tremor in the ferns.

We climbed into the car and started back to Government House. Even the artificial breeze from our speed was a relief, although one could tell nothing from that, of course. Out of the window I watched the tops of palms against the sky, and, as we crossed a river, the small boats ("close-hauled on the edge of the wind—"). But they were not close-hauled. Their sails were slack and dimpled untidily, making no headway. There was no wind. The dust on the road, the smoke from distant huts, the ripples in a marsh—everything, I watched. And finally I was looking at the limp flag, wrapped around the pole outside of Government House. We were back again.

I spoke at last, like a sick person who can no longer control his obsession.

"I am afraid there is very little wind this evening," I said, dry-mouthed.

"Oh, you can't tell from here," said the Governor's wife, anxiously, "we'll go down to the pier and look."

We hurried across the road and walked out over the water. It felt cooler there but the bay was glassy. I held up my hand.

"No, there isn't a breath of wind," I said.

"There is a *little*," said the Governor's wife, "but I can't tell from where." She turned to face the harbor mouth.

I pulled out my handkerchief. "We can see," I said, "if there is any—" The handkerchief hung down limply, swinging slightly from my hand. "No, there isn't enough to lift a handkerchief." And to myself I thought, what a heavy thing a handkerchief is!

We walked back across the road.

"You see, it's our last chance tonight," I said, "tomorrow the moon won't be bright enough. If we can't get off tonight—well, we'll just have to change our plans."

"But you can't tell yet," urged the Governor's wife kindly, "the wind may come up after sunset."

"Yes, of course," I said, but I did not feel hopeful. I went up to my room and tried to write, to read, to rest.

Listen! the wind is rising,
and the air—

But it wasn't rising. It was completely dead.
Why did I learn that poem? I couldn't get it out
of my head now. It would taunt me the rest of the
evening. It would go on singing inanely in my
head no matter what happened. Calm yourself.
Learn something else, something quieting. Get
out the little scrapbook.

Brave flowers—that I could gallant it like you,
And be as little vain!
You come abroad, and make a harmless show— [1]

No, that was too difficult. It would never come
to you in a crisis. Only the first line rolled out
like a banner:

Brave flowers—that I could gallant it like you—

Fifteen minutes, a half-hour, three-quarters
passed. It was after sunset. I could stay in no
longer. I would go out to the pier again. You
couldn't tell, sometimes everything changed in a
second and started rolling the right way. It might
be happening right now. This might be the very
second, the knife edge, when the wind changed.
It would do no harm to go and see.

I slipped out of my room quietly and walked
in a firm taut step down the stairs and through

[1] Henry King, "A Contemplation upon Flowers."

the halls—the kind of step you used in a dream
when you wished to hurry from the person behind, but it would be fatal to run. Down the steps
of Government House, out of the driveway. Not
in a hurry at all, just a nice brisk walk. Once out
in the road, I could clip along faster; it was dark.
And when I reached the pier, I was running, my
feet clumping down the board-walk. Yes, it was
cooler, definitely cooler, but— ("Sister Anne,
Sister Anne, do you see anyone coming?" Old
fairy tales, old rhymes, raced through my mind.
"Flounder, Flounder, in the sea!") was there a
wind? I took out my handkerchief, crumpled
whiteness in the dark. It hung from my hand; it
swayed; it fluttered; it pulled gently away from
me. It leaned upon a breath of air. Yes, yes, it
had changed! Oh—"Listen! the wind is rising,
and the air—"

I ran back to Government House and burst
into the room. My husband had just come back
from the bay.

"The wind has changed," I panted, out of
breath, "I've just been down to the pier. There's
enough to lift a handkerchief!"

"Good," he said, "I'll go down with you and
see."

We walked down side by side, across the road
again, I pushing my steps ahead to keep up with
his long ones. Yes, there was a wind. Two hand-

kerchiefs fluttered from the pier. It occurred to me, an aftermath to my excitement, that a wind that could lift a handkerchief might not be able to lift a plane. Still, it was a good sign. There was definitely a change. And there might be more when the moon came up.

We went back to dinner. The Governor toasted our success. I wondered—for the third time—if that would be the last. We said good-by.

"We'll probably see you at breakfast, though," we laughed in bravado.

The Governor's wife squeezed both my hands.

"Send us a cable, will you, when you get there?" said the Governor. (Casual, taking it for granted. How British—how grand of him!)

"Yes, we will, good-by, thank you."

We walked out to the pier again. The moon was up, low and reddish on the horizon, and terribly squashed in, since last night. It looked lopsided and bruised, like a misshapen pear. I was shocked. How fast it changed. This was certainly the last night we could use it. But the wind was a little stronger. That helped.

We went back to the house. There was nothing more to do. Our things, a small handful only, were rolled into the bottom of the white canvas sack. The rest of our clothes lay on the pile of discarded equipment. My husband took only the suit he was wearing. I had, besides my flying clothes, one silk dress, a pair of stockings and a linen hat, wound up in a roll. Altogether we had about twelve ounces in the bottom of the white sack. It was tucked away now. We were ready to go.

But we could not leave until the moon was high; we needed all the light we could get for our take-off. We lay down and waited for the minutes to pass. The house was still. Everyone else had settled for the night. It had not started for us—not yet. Wait, wait, wait—my heart hammered in my throat:

> with all adventure before them—
> with all adventure . . .

At ten-twenty the tall house-boy, Samiker, knocked on the door for our luggage. Luggage? We had none. Only the half-empty white sack, my radio bag, an extra shirt and sweater, and the helmets. He shouldered the limp bag silently and went out. The small open car was at the door. We climbed in the back quietly. Samiker jumped in after us. It wasn't necessary for him to come, but I was glad because I felt he cared. And it was nice to have around you people who cared, even if they said nothing. We started off. Radio bag? Helmets? Lunch? Yes. Samiker sat in front with the white sack. We bumped through the dimly lighted streets. People were closing up for the night. Someone pushed open a shutter above our heads, as we passed, and leaned down out of a lighted window to see what it was. Oh, I thought —looking up for one flashing second at the bright window, at the dark hand stretched out carelessly to draw back the shutters—oh, if only it were as casual as that to us!

The car sighed to a stop in front of the closed gates. The sleepy guard came out and let us through. ("Listen! the wind is rising—" There was not a breath, not a breath on shore.) We climbed into the leaky rowboat. Samiker sat down behind us with the white sack. The water sucked and slopped around our feet. (—and the air is wild with leaves"—no wind—no wind.) The boy at the oars coughed painfully. We pushed slowly ahead toward the indistinct form of the plane.

There was a fair light from the moon. I could see the captain of the port sitting in a small rowboat near us. There was more wind out here. I turned my head to let it blow back my hair.

"There's as much wind as the morning we tried before, Charles," I said as we touched the side of the plane.

"But not as much as the night?" He climbed out of the boat.

"No—I had on my sweater that night."

We started to arrange the cockpits, to pump out the pontoons, those endless small jobs we had done so many times before. But tonight, it was the last time, they took on an incredible importance. They were lit with an intensity of feeling and stood out like the smallest branches of trees at night in a bright crack of lightning. I knelt on the nose of the pontoon and held the flashlight while my husband pumped. The water sloshed out in regular gasps. "All right, now, the anchor box." Words, too, seemed weighted beyond their usual freight of feeling. He took some putty and worked it with his fingers along the edges of the hatch. "That ought to keep the water out." The circle of light followed his fingers as they moved, deftly and swiftly up and down.

It was very still. I drummed with my fingernails on the light metal under me. *"First* in *war— First* in *peace—First* in the *hearts* of his *count*ree *men:"* my fingernails beat out the rhythm in the stillness. Ping ping ping; ping ping ping. Was there no other sound? Listen, listen, listen— listen, the wind is rising—

My husband looked up from his work. "There's about a five-mile wind right now," he called across the water.

The captain of the port held up his hand in the dim moonlight. "You air-folk must look at it differently," he drawled back good-naturedly.

"Why? What would you call it?" We stopped

bolt still, and listened. ("—and the air is wild with leaves—")

"Almost a dead calm!"

We laughed and bent over the pontoons again. Ping, ping, ping. Ping, ping, ping, *"First* in the *hearts* of his *count*ree *men."*

But there *was* more wind, I thought, as I climbed into the cockpit. There was enough for me to put my sweater on. "Charles, there's enough wind for me to put my sweater on!" But he could not hear. He was untying the lantern, now the bridle.

"If we come back, we'll want these," he said, "otherwise—" The end of his sentence was lost in the moonlight, like the shores, like the trees.

He stood up to say good-by. "Well, we'll have another try."

He swung up into the cockpit. He started the engine.

I felt under my feet for obstructions; saw that the control wires were free; sat on my extra shirt, stuffed the lunch in the aluminum case; put the radio bag in the seat beside me. There now, fasten the belt. Ready.

We pushed out into the bay. It was not such a strange world tonight. We had been here before. I greeted old landmarks. There were the lights of the town. There was the path of the moon.

(—where the ships of youth are running
　　close-hauled on the edge of the wind—)

If only there were a wind. There was more out
in the bay, but it was not as rough as the other
night. Still, we were about two hundred pounds
lighter. We taxied over our take-off stretch. We
tried out the engine; we throttled down; we swung
into the wind. That pause for breath. The last
look out: the palms outlined dimly above the
town; the moon, a bright path ahead; and the
wind—the wind was rising—

"All set?"

"All right."

Here we go. Hold on. The roar, the spray over
the wings. Look at your watch. Won't be more
than two minutes. Then you'll know. You can
stand two minutes. Look at your watch. That's
your job. Listen—listen—the spray has stopped.
We are spanking along. We are up on the step
—faster, faster—oh, much faster than before.
Sparks from the exhaust. We're going to get off!
But how long it takes. Spank, spank—we're off?
Not yet—spank—almost. Splutter, choke—the engine? My God—it's coming then—death. He's going on just the same. We're off—no more spanks.
Splutter—splutter. What is wrong? Will he turn?
Will we land? The wobble pump? Gas? Mixture?
Never mind, your job, the watch. Just two, Green-

wich. Yes—we're off—we're rising. But why start off with an engine like that?

But it smooths out now, like a long sigh, like a person breathing easily, freely. Like someone singing ecstatically, climbing, soaring—sustained note of power and joy. We turn from the lights of the city; we pivot on a dark wing; we roar over the earth. The plane seems exultant now, even arrogant. We did it, we did it! We're up, above you. We were dependent on you just now, River, prisoners fawning on you for favors, for wind and light. But now, we are free. We are up; we are off. We can toss you aside, you there, way below us, a few lights in the great dark silent world that is ours—for we are above it.

PART 3

BOUND NATAL

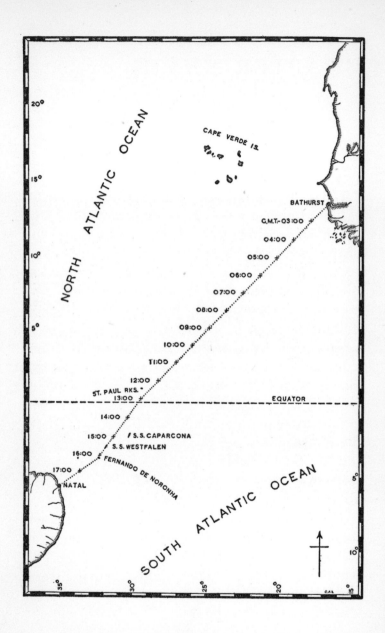

NORTH ATLANTIC OCEAN

CAPE VERDE IS.

BATHURST

G.M.T.—03:00
04:00
05:00
06:00
07:00
08:00
09:00
10:00
11:00
12:00
ST. PAUL RKS. ·   13:00   EQUATOR
14:00
15:00   / S.S. CAPARCONA
16:00   S.S. WESTFALEN
17:00   FERNANDO DE NORONHA
NATAL

SOUTH ATLANTIC OCEAN

20°
15°
10°
5°

5°
10°

35°   30°   25°   20°   15°

CHAPTER XXVIII

MY LITTLE ROOM ·

THE lights flashed on in the front cockpit, outlining my husband's head and shoulders. Then off again quickly. He was looking at the chart. We turned low over the shadowy land. I reached up and wrenched back the sliding cockpit cover, shutting out the noise and wind. The papers in my lap stopped fluttering wildly. I took out my large pad. Still taut from excitement, I wrote down by moonlight, "Took off Bathurst 2:00 GMT." Looking at the sentence scrawled unevenly across the top of the big sheet of blank paper, I said sternly to myself, "Well, you needn't get so excited— After all, we've got the whole flight ahead of us. Heaven knows if we'll get there." But I could not help feeling that the worst was over, now we were off, that after this all would be easy.

It was just as well, however, to be pulled down to practical affairs. There was no time now for fear or exaltation, for speculation or doubt. The windless bay, the docks, the lights, the palm trees, had dropped off behind us. I was concerned with them no longer. Neither was the great dark world outside my cockpit cover any business of mine. The moon, the stars, the wind, the formless stretch of land we were crossing, the vast ocean we were headed toward—all these I must shut out. For me they did not exist. All that existed now was this small cockpit, pulled over me like the shell of a snail. From now on until we reached the other side of the ocean, there I should stay curled down, oblivious to the outside world, touching it only through those faint squeaks in the earphones, through the light taps of my fingers.

It is strange how one's place of work, anywhere, becomes an all-important world—how it becomes, even more than that, a shelter and a home, enclosing and buttressing you on all sides, giving you a sense of security, no matter how precarious it may actually be—even hurtling blindly through the air.

This little cockpit of mine became extraordinarily pleasing to me, as much so as a furnished study at home. Every corner, every crack, had significance. Every object meant something. Not only the tools I was working with, the transmitter and receiver, the key and the antenna reel; but even the small irrelevant objects on the side of the fuselage, the little black hooded light, its face now turned away from me, the shining arm and knob of the second throttle, the bright switches and handles, the colored wires and copper pipes: all gave me, in a strange sense, as much pleasure as my familiar books and pictures might at home. The pleasure was perhaps not esthetic but came from a sense of familiarity, security, and possession. I invested them with an emotional significance of their own, since they had been through so much with me. They made up this comfortable, familiar, tidy, compact world that was mine.

There were, in the first place, the oval sides of the fuselage, curving up around me in a way that was curiously comforting and secure. They seemed to surround me in a warmer, more friendly fashion than the straight inanimate walls of a room, so that I felt as snug as a bird in a nest.

There was my curved metal seat, securely rooted in the floor, wide and comfortable with its creased leather cushion. When I was not flying the plane, or bent over the receiver, I could squat, kneel, or curl up in it. There was plenty of room besides, in the corners, for my radio bag, an extra sweater or two, a package of sandwiches, pencils, pads, mittens, coils that I was changing—everything, in fact, that I needed. It was the only safe place to put things, where I could keep my hands on them, and be sure nothing would get lost or fall down on the floor. I was always afraid that a lunch box or a coil would get wedged in the controls and cause an accident. The seat would bounce up or bump down as I pulled a cable underneath. I preferred it down so that I could work at the receiver. And when down, I was completely buried in the cockpit, only the top of my head, my eyes and nose emerging. It was, of course, the center of my world and seemed much more than a seat to me. It attained the importance of that special armchair, or bed, or corner, which is to a child his ship or his house.

Directly in front of me, between my legs, was the aluminum stick, with its corrugated rubber cap on top to grip. I could twist this out of its socket and fasten it into a clamp at the side when I was operating radio, as it interfered with the pad on my lap. In front of the stick was the box holding the sextant, which slid into grooves fastened to the floor. On either side of the sextant box were the rudders. At my right hand was the board which held the shiny black sending key, and the drift-meter with its eye-piece to peer down at the waves below.

On the right side of the cockpit, about the height of my knees, was the receiver, a long narrow black box, mounted on springs and sponge rubber. In smooth air, its top served as a temporary shelf for notes and sandwiches passed between my husband and myself, although it was rather unsafe, and things were apt to jiggle off onto the floor. When operating the radio, as the box was rather low, I had to bend way over in order to watch and adjust the dials. At the same time, I had to keep a pad balanced on my lap for taking down messages. Receiving was still quite difficult. Except for familiar words and expressions, I could not yet translate the messages in my head and was forced to write them letter by letter as the sounds came to my ear. My pencil and not my mind apparently did the translating, hopping busily across the page. When the pencil stopped I would look down and see what had been written.

At the right side of the seat, out of sight but well within reach, was the box for the transmitter coils. The transmitter itself, a square black box, mounted like the receiver, was in front of me on my left. Its door let down and formed a convenient ledge for the coils as I was changing them. Then there was the antenna reel on the floor below this, its copper wire running down through a hole in the foot-boards. When we took off, this was wound up tightly, the ball-weight on the end pulled snugly against the outside of the fair-lead. But once we were up, it trailed in the air behind us.

A constant worry of mine was lest we lose the ball-weight on the end of the antenna. It could easily be snapped off by a sudden impact with the water if we landed unexpectedly, or flew too near the surface of the waves before I had time to reel in. This had happened to me once before in an emergency landing at night in Alaska. I remembered quite well frantically winding the handle with an aching arm, racing against the descent of the plane; then the ominous jerk as the ball-weight spun off into the sea; and, as I continued to wind, the unaccustomed lightness with which the frayed end of wire snapped back airily into the cockpit. For such a contingency there was an extra weight in the repair box in my husband's cockpit.

At my left shoulder, fastened to the side of the fuselage, was the aluminum map-case. It is odd, but flyers always have the most ungrateful feelings about map-cases. No matter how ample the designers make them, they never seem anything but stingy in size. You cannot get all the maps into them or, if you can, you can never wrench them out again without tearing the edges. Perhaps it was because I used to put everything besides maps into mine; radio pamphlets, lists, sandwiches, helmet, and pencils. This one always had a screw out and the flap slightly stretched from the wall. The screw, together with other small nameless screws, washers, bits of grit, crumbs and dust, which gathered there, danced perpetually in a tiny whirlwind of vibration on the floor in a corner of the cockpit just out of my reach.

Looking forward, mid-way between my husband's cockpit and mine, and slightly raised from the floor, was the aperiodic compass, the one instrument I could clearly see and fly by, watching its swinging parallel white lines and figures as I pushed the rudders. Then, ahead, was my husband's cockpit. I could see him, his back at least, in segments; his helmet above the cockpit, through our sliding covers. Then, through the cockpit itself, his shoulder and arm, the shiny black back of his seat, the duralumin tubes on which it slid up and down, and the V-shaped rubber cords that helped support it. Although he was only a few inches from me, communication was not easy. He could turn around and shout back to me but I could never, even with the wildest shriek, make myself heard above the engine's roar. I would write little notes, poke my husband in the back with a pencil (the degree of poke depending on my state of excitement) and pass him the paper, firmly held so it would not blow out of the cockpit.

But it was not only by sight that my little room was known to me. It was even more intimately known by touch. Everything was within arm's reach (except the toy-typhoon of screws). Everything obeyed my hand: the stick which twisted down into the socket in the floor, the edges of whose rubber handle I had dog-eared fondly; the rudders, answering to one's feet like stirrups; but also, more personally mine, the little round flat disk, that was my radio key. Smooth and polished as a counter, it fitted lightly between my fingers, as comfortable, as familiar, as a pencil; obedient as any tool, and, as a tool, giving one a sense of pleasure to use it, play with it, master it, ride it.

Without sight, my fingers also knew the precise shape and spin of the small screws to open the radio boxes. My hand knew the plump smooth wooden handle of the antenna reel, and the cold square metal brake to fasten it. I could even change the coils by touch alone, running my finger over the polished spool and the ribbed surface of tightly wound wires, judging by the number of turns the wave-length of the coil.

Tonight, I must do all by touch. The moonlight, which bloomed luminous on my white pad and dimly outlined the objects in the cockpit, did not brush into the darkest corners, did not throw any more light on the coil-box or the antenna reel. And though I could switch on the little hooded light, and might need to later on, to read by, I did not want to use it while we were still over land. The artificial glow might reflect into the front cockpit and take away some fraction of my husband's meager vision. Flying on the night mail, he once told me, I remembered, that the dimmest light in the cockpit might blind you temporarily.

I ran my fingers over the coils, found the right ones, jiggled them out of their places and pressed them (smelling faintly of shellac) into their sockets in the transmitter box. I clamped down the earphones over my ears. I switched on the receiver. The luminous dials glowed warmly out of the dark. I reached for the plump handle of the antenna reel. I put my fingers on the smooth key. "Darr dit darr dit, dit darr dit -" My work had begun. Outside the night rushed by. How nice to be in your own little room, to pull your belongings around you, to draw in like a snail in his shell, to work!

CHAPTER XXIX

THE NIGHT

"CRKK   CRKK [Porto Praia] DE KHCAL [The call letters of our plane]." It was 2:15. I had just time to call Porto Praia before my regular hourly and half-hourly schedule with the Pan American stations on the coast of South America. The heavy dragging buzz of my own sending rang closely in my ears. Then silence. Listening, fingering the bright dials in the darkness of the cockpit. No answer. Only the crashes of static in my earphones. I tried again. No answer. Perhaps he never got the telegram, I thought, on that timeless island. What time was it, anyway? Two-fifteen, Greenwich; one-fifteen, here. It was the middle of the night, of course. Why *should* he be watching for us? He was asleep; the radio house on the top of the hill was empty.

I reeled in the antenna. I changed the coils. I reeled out for another resonance point on another wave. I would start calling the Pan American stations on the coast; not that I expected to get an answer as early as this, but simply because we had agreed to send on the hour and half-hour. It was now two-thirty.

"PVC   PVC [Ceara] DE KHCAL." No answer, except the crashes of static, from that outer world. For to put on your earphones and tap into the radio waves is to open a window to another world, to have a peephole to the outside, an earhole. Tonight it was a very different world from the one in which I was sitting. Here all was still, snug and ordered. My husband sat calmly at the controls; I was curled up in my seat. Moonlight bathed the cabin; the night was clear; the plane bored its way steadily through a cloudless sky. But out there, in that outer cosmos, so it seemed to me listening, worlds were crashing; planets were breaking up. I could hear the tossing and hurling, the cracking and breaking, the terror and night.

Frightful static, I thought to myself, I wonder what that means— Storms? And I made a note on my fluttering featherweight radio pad: "Nil hrd [Nothing heard] QRN [Atmospherics]." No, I couldn't hear anything through that, but I might as well send out "blind" our time of take-off. Someone might pick it up, even though there didn't seem much chance. It was like putting a message into a corked bottle and throwing it overboard in a storm.

"PVC   PVC DE KHCAL   TOOK OFF BATHURST 02:00 GMT."

No answer in the earphones, only those stars clashing in the distance, those moons cart-wheeling through space. For you seem to hear distance and space on the radio. Sounds punctuate the silence, like stars the dark, giving you a sense of perspective.

But I was beginning to hear something else besides the cosmic crashes, faint squeaks against the welter of noise, precise scratchings upon the blurred surface of sound. So dim and faint, they were no more than a twig's tapping on a window-pane during a storm; no more than a crab's track on sand, partly erased by a wave; or a dead leaf's tracing on new-fallen snow. They were living, however; they were human, I was sure. They were dot-dash, Morse-code letters, words, messages of a human being.

I put my pencil on the page and let it jot down stray letters where I thought I could hear them between crashes: "O - - - - T - - - - C - - - FN - - - R - - - - K - - - L." Then suddenly, through the welter of sounds, I heard no longer letters but my name, or so it sounded to me, KHCAL, the call letters of the plane. Across an ocean and through the night, my name! More thrilling than to hear your nickname in a room full of strangers, or your own language in a street of foreigners. Someone was calling us, an ocean away. Someone had heard us—in our little cabin, flying in the dark in a plane thousands of miles away. Who was it?

"SORRY CAN'T COPY   QRS [Please send more slowly]," I answered and pressed the phones to my ears.

"Dit darr dit - dit darr dit [R—received OK]," I heard dimly through the crashes. Then, "PVB BAHIA."

PVB, Pan American station at Bahia, South America. Right on the watch—good man! I switched on the light and poked my husband in the back with a pencil (rather excitedly I am afraid, for he jumped) and handed him a note.

"Can *just* hear PVB, Bahia, but think he hears me OK. Have you any msg [message]?"

He sent back *"Very* good" with his first message which I tapped out firmly, double-sending, across the ocean to Bahia.

"TOOK OFF 2:00 GMT [Greenwich Mean Time]
  POSN [Position at] 3:00 GMT
  12° 17′ N
  17° 50′ W
  COURSE 224° TRUE"

"Dit darr dit - dit darr dit [R—received OK]," came back the faint clicks. He got it! Over two thousand miles away. We really were in contact with South America. We had jumped the distance, touched hands between hemispheres.

I felt as though the voyage were now not unguided. A path had opened up through the night. There was our goal. Hitherto it had been unseen, unheard, theoretical. It was a point on a compass, a dot on a map, convincing enough to my husband, but to me, not nearly as tangible as this—this faint, fluctuating, but friendly eye of a distant lighthouse.

From now on through three hours of night, I sat hunched over the lighted dials. Only once did I look out, a brief backward glance which told me we were well out over the water, for there, in the vast darkness underneath, were the twinkling lights of a ship far below us. How long would it be until I saw another boat, I thought in passing, and turned quickly back to my work. My hand on the knobs, the earphones pressed close against my ears, I sat straining to hear through the crashes of static. It was maddening. You could almost hear, almost, and then a crash would blot out everything. It was like trying to find something in the dark by lighting little matches whose flare petered out just as you were about to put your hand down. Or like trying to pick up a shell in the glossy smooth stretch of sand in the tail of a receiving wave. Before you could quite get there another wave crashed over.

I reeled in and out the antenna; I changed coils; I tapped out positions, repeating twice,

three times, over and over again for the man at
the other end who was also straining to hear.

"POSN 4:00 GMT

   11° 05' N

   19° 05' W

   COURSE 224° TRUE

   1/10 OVERCAST AT 2000 FEET   VISIBILITY

   UNLIMITED   WIND 10 KNOTS 30°   ALTI-

   TUDE 1200 FEET   MAKING 100 KNOTS."

I did not dare look up. In that half-second some
whisper in the air might escape me. But I could
tell it was still good weather by the moonlight
over my shoulder. By this light I would write
and send my own messages. I had to switch on
the cabin-light for receiving, which was literally
a kind of deciphering of hieroglyphics my pencil
had automatically jotted down on the page. What
could I glean from those scattered letters? At first,
nothing, a few stray words only of the weather reports they were trying to send me: "MOON - - -
WIND - - NORTHEAST." Then gradually more. After
much repetition I got some weather from Rio.
(PVB, Bahia had "passed me on" to Rio.) Things
were going better. I breathed more easily,
stretched myself and looked at my watch. Almost
five—three hours since we took off—we were over
three hundred miles out over the Atlantic—could
it be possible! I felt as if I had hardly caught my
breath, hardly stopped to realize we were off, on

our way to South America. Relaxing a little, I realized also that I was very tired. I was sending with my eyes closed.

"POSN 5:00 GMT
  09° 50′ N
  20° 15′ W
  COURSE 224° TRUE
  9/10 OVERCAST   VISIBILITY 10 MILES
  WIND 10 KNOTS 30°   ALTITUDE 1200."

It was a rest to send. Sleepy already, and I had the whole day to go through! But that would be *day*. Night was the hardest. It would be all right once it was day, I kept saying. (Just as I had said in Bathurst, it will be all right once we get off.)

We began to hit clouds. I could tell without looking up, for the plane bumped slightly from time to time, first one wing down and then the other. And the moon blackened out for short periods. Then for longer periods. I could not see to write my messages. I stiffened, dimly sensing fear—the old fear of bad weather—and looked out. We were flying under clouds. I could still find a kind of horizon, a difference in shading where the water met the clouds. That was all. But it seemed to be getting darker. Storms? Were those clouds or was it the sky? We had lost the water. We were flying blind. I turned off the light quickly (to give my husband a little more vision), and sat waiting, tense, peering through the night.

Now we were out again. There were holes through which one could see the dark water, and holes through which one could see the dark sky. It was all right, I felt, as long as there were holes.

More blind flying. This is it, I thought, this is what people forget. This is what it means to fly across an ocean, blind and at night. But day is coming. It ought to be day before long. I tried to figure out—one hour off Greenwich. When did the sun rise? In an hour? Could we go through this for an hour?

We were climbing up through the clouds. The static hissed in my ears. I could not see the pad to write and I did not seem able to control my fingers to send steadily. But I must keep contact. "QRX - QRX [Please stand by]" I sent out, postponing my usual contact, "GOING THRU CLOUDS - MIN PSE [Please wait a minute]." We came out into the stars. My hand steadied. "QRX - ALL OK," I sent blindly. Again clouds ahead; again blind flying; again we were climbing. I was shivering. It was cold, that was it; we were higher. Never let yourself get cold when you're frightened, I reminded myself, it just makes it worse.

I put on my extra shirt and tried to work again. But I could not read my messages in pitch blackness, and I did not dare turn on the light. It might make it harder to fly. "QRX - QRX - ALL OK."

A slip of paper was scratching my knee. My

husband had pushed back a note, a message to send. I switched on the light.

"8/10 overcast," I read. "Scattered squalls— Visibility 3 miles— Daybreak."

Daybreak! what a miracle. I didn't see any sign of day and yet it must be lighter. The clouds were distinguishing themselves more and more from water and sea.

Daybreak—thank God—as if we had been living in eternal night—as if this were the first sun that ever rose out of the sea.

CHAPTER XXX

A DISTANT LIGHTHOUSE

"POSN 7:00 GMT [Five hours gone now.]
  07° 25' N
  22° 30' W
  COURSE 224° TRUE
  9/10 OVERCAST AT 1000   FREQUENT SQUALLS
  VISIBILITY UNLIMITED AWAY FROM SQUALLS
  SEA CALM   WIND ZERO."

At the word *unlimited,* I looked up. Lovely word, which opens like a window from the straight walls of a radio report. How often, standing in some station on a wet field, with the sky a gray and lowering curtain, listening to the weather reports coming in from the west, I had waited for that word. "Newark—Newark—overcast—local storms," the monotonous voice on the radio would drone out. "Sunbury—Sunbury—visibility two miles—" (Down on the mountains.) "Bellefonte—lower broken clouds—ceiling estimated 3,000 feet." (That's better.) "Cleveland—Cleveland—ceiling and visibility unlimited—" (Good—we could go!)

Unlimited, my breath quickens at the sound of

it. For it suggests more than the technically perfect, "ceiling and visibility unlimited." It calls up pictures of a soft wide cloudless sky, the morning of an endless summer day, a smooth and rippleless sea, spread silken to the horizon.

Not that this was the picture I saw now, looking out of the cockpit, but still, the weather was definitely better. Or perhaps it was the light. I could see the clouds that we had been going through, black pillowy thunderclouds that we grazed under, bumping heavily. They stretched out on all sides, a dark curtain pressing down on our heads. But underneath you could see clearly; and beyond, it looked brighter. Yes—"visibility unlimited"—now everything would be easy.

The radio was better, too. I was hearing well enough to receive, through triple-sending and a good deal of repetition, a message from Rio about the landing arrangements at Natal. It seemed incredible to think about landing when we were more than half an ocean away. Yet there was the message on my pad. It read like a professional telegram:

"RIO JANEIRO   DECEMBER 6TH   LINDBERGHS KHCAL   PAA BARGE AT NATAL [Would we ever really get there?] LOCATED ON RIVER AT SOUTHWEST EDGE OF CITY STOP BETWEEN CITY AND LARGE AERO POSTALE HANGAR AND RAMP STOP [As though finding it would be any difficulty once we were there.]

CAUTION TALL RADIO MASTS AT AERO POSTALE
HANGAR STOP [Caution! radio masts in full day-
light—caution—after that moonlight take-off!]
FEW SPARE PARTS AVAILABLE ON BARGE."

"Few spare parts available." They evidently
did expect us at the other end. The very attention
to details seemed to bring the goal nearer. Natal
began to materialize before my eyes. I felt light-
hearted. I ate one of my sandwiches. I began writing cheerful notes to my husband. There had not
been time before this.

"I still can't believe we got off." I wrote excitedly, "What was all that spluttering?"

"Insufficient gas feed," he scribbled back.

"I thought motor failure on take-off! Will we
get out of the storms by and by?" ran my next
question.

"By and by," was his noncommittal answer.

"I think you are wonderful," I added in a
burst of enthusiasm.

The only comment on this last item was a heavy
pencil mark. It looked like a firm laconic check.

Well—it was all wonderful, the take-off, the day,
and the weather. I did not even mind the storms.
I rather enjoyed bumping under the clouds. It
was like a mild roller-coaster, and added to my
general good spirits. The sky grew brighter; I
tapped out messages regularly.

"POSN 8:00 GMT [Six hours behind us, now.]
06° 15′ N
23° 40′ W
COURSE 224° TRUE
9/10 OVERCAST AT 1500   FREQUENT SQUALLS
VISIBILITY UNLIMITED OUTSIDE SQUALLS   SEA
CALM   WIND ZERO   ALTITUDE 1000."

Suddenly, in the middle of my usual contact with Rio, I heard a loud note barging in over the radio, like heavy clumping footsteps filling the air. Who was it, knocking on my door?

"KHCAL DE WCC."

WCC—I couldn't believe it! WCC was thousands of miles away. It was that big station in Massachusetts. I looked it up to make sure. Yes, Chatham, Massachusetts, was calling us.

"ANSWER [on] 36 [meters] OR 54 [meters]," went on the heavy voice.

Could it be Chatham, Massachusetts, as loud as that? It was completely unreal. But the whole night was unreal, so I answered quite casually on 57 meters (the wave-length I was using), not bothering to change to the shorter wave.

He answered immediately, the notes pounding through, clear and strong, every word intact. I did not need his triple-sending but hardly dared interrupt. Chatham, Massachusetts, nearly four thousand miles away—think how thrilling!

Slowly the message dribbled onto the page:
"WOULD YOU ANSWER ANSWER ANSWER FEW FEW

FEW QUESTIONS QUESTIONS QUESTIONS FIRST RADIO
INTERVIEW FROM FROM FROM AIRPLANE."

Newspapers here too, out in the middle of the
ocean—what a disappointment. My thrilling contact with Chatham was just an interview. It was
like a dream in which the door knob slowly turns
into a grinning face. The night was more unreal
than ever now.

"SORRY," I tapped back, "TOO BUSY HERE
MUST GET WEATHER FROM PVJ."

Had I lost PVJ in the excitement? I began calling him insistently, reeling in and out the antenna and changing coils. Finally, I heard him
faintly on 36 (meters) and sent out hurriedly our
last position.

"POSN 09:00 GMT
 05° 00′ N
 24° 45′ W
 COURSE 224° TRUE
 2/10 OVERCAST AT 1500   9/10 OVERCAST
 AT 8000   VISIBILITY   UNLIMITED   SEA
 CALM   WIND ZERO   ALTITUDE 1200."

Yes, he got it; now for the weather from Natal.

"WEA [weather] NATAL - - - ," he started to give
me in return. But the rest of his message faded
out, smothered in silence. I pressed my earphones
against my head; I bent over the dials; I could
not hear it. The game of blindman's-buff had
started again.

CHAPTER XXXI

THE DAY

TEN o'clock—eight hours behind us, eight ahead; we were halfway. By now the sun was well up at our back. The day was good. There were no more storms, only a few clouds left wandering at our own level. And far above, the sky was a broken overcast. Bits of blue showed through its gray folds. The sea below, rippled with little waves, looked peaceful and calm as far as one could see. It was still "unlimited."

But I was very tired, the thought of the whole day ahead seemed an unbearable burden. I was sending all the time now with my eyes closed. To open them again to write was like lifting day and night. Time, in hours, minutes, and seconds, like an ever-increasing weight of sand, piled on my lids. Sleep settled on me like a fall of feathers. One more feather and I should go under, be drowned in that delicious sea.

Now, you *mustn't* go to sleep, I would shake myself. Suppose the pilot went to sleep at the controls? You must keep contact.

But there was nothing on the radio to keep me awake. All sounds had faded out. Sleep seemed to have fallen, also, on that outer world. Even the crashes of static had disappeared. I would have been glad even to hear them. Anything but this still death-like cotton-wool void, in which no creature was alive but me.

I changed the coils, I reeled in and out the antenna. I tapped out my positions "blind," hoping that the Pan American stations at the other end could hear me even if I could not hear them (which, in fact, was the case). But I could wake no reply.

"NIL HRD [nothing heard] ON 36

POSN 10:00 GMT

04° 00′ N

26° 00′ W

9/10 OVERCAST   VISIBILITY UNLIMITED

SEA CALM   WIND 10 KNOTS 135°   ALTI-

TUDE 800."

Perhaps I *was* asleep, I thought at times, and that was why I couldn't hear anything. I certainly was not very quick at turning the dials and changing the coils. My back ached from that perpetually bent-over position and my ears hurt from the clamp of the phones. (I had fastened my helmet over the phones and pulled it down tightly, hoping to shut out all outside noise and pin myself more closely to the radio world.) **My** thumb and finger, too, had sore dents in them from pressing the key too hard in my intensity. None of these things was difficult in itself. They were trifling annoyances, easily overlooked or overcome by a little will-power. But when you are very tired your will is tired too. It seems to go more quickly than the mind. My thoughts were clear; I knew what I should do but it did not seem worth the effort.

Come now, you must do something about this, I would say to myself.

Yes, but what? Nothing I do will help. It takes all the strength I have just to stay where I am.

Well, try something, anyway, even if you don't think it will do any good. First get the canteen, a drink of water. A little on the handkerchief to wipe off your face. Then a sandwich.

It *did* help, surprisingly, and I felt more awake. But the radio was as dead as ever.

"NIL HRD ON 36   PSE [please] GO 53."

In the middle of my efforts I got a note from my husband. He would like to take some "sun sights" with the sextant, to check our position. Would I fly for a while?

I certainly would. I put my pad away and jiggled the stick into its socket on the floor between my legs. If I couldn't contact anyone on the radio, I might as well make myself useful some other way. I straightened up to the stick, I stretched my legs out to meet the rudders, pushing them gently this way and that. What a relief to change my position, to push, to do something active.

It was pleasant to look out, too. We were skimming along near the water. The sea was mottled, now, with sunshine and deep purple shadows. The gray overcast curtain above had broken into big loose white clouds, piled up in a bright blue sky. My eye wandered from the brightness of the clouds to the dark shadows of the cockpit, where the compass stood on the floor ahead of me. That swinging arrow must be kept parallel to the white lines if we were to continue straight on our course. And the ship must be steady while my husband held the sextant to his eye. My hands stiffened on the stick, my feet on the rudders. Now please, I would think, trying to wheedle the plane like a pony, don't buck or kick for a few minutes.

I left my earphones on and the antenna trailing, so that in between the "sights" I could try to contact stations. The sun was over our heads, hot on our backs. The middle of the day. A deep noonday sleep still swathed the radio. I sent out our position "blind" again.

"POSN 11:00 GMT [Nine hours behind us; seven
to go.]
02° 50′ N
27° 10′ W
COURSE 224° TRUE
6/10 OVERCAST AT 10000   VISIBILITY UN-
LIMITED   SEA LIGHT   WIND 10 KNOTS 135°
ALTITUDE 800."

There was no answer. "Nil hrd on 36—nil hrd
on 54—Nil hrd 600 to 900—nil—nil," were the
notes on my pad.

How about the sights? I peered forward at my
husband and tried to read his face. He did not
look satisfied. Was he working out calculations
on his pad? No, he was taking the sextant to
pieces on his lap! Something had gone wrong
then; the sights were no good. We were over
halfway across and it was vital to have radio. I
reeled out again.

"PVJ   PVJ   DE KHCAL."

I swept the dial. *There*—yes, there *was* a squeak.
There were some signals, an answer.

"KHCAL [But it wasn't PVJ, a different note, a
different place on the dial.] DE CRKK."

CRKK—Porto Praia, behind us! Now farther
away than the South American stations. Was it
the "Chef," I wondered, sitting up in the radio
shack? It might, of course, be that pale little oper-

ator. But I thought not. Somehow, I was con-
vinced it was the "Chef" in his loose gray coat.
He *had* received the telegram and was "on watch"
for us. "WE LISTEN YOU ALL TIME," he had once
said. "POSN PSE [Please give position]," he asked
now.

"POSN 12:00 GMT [Ten hours passed; six ahead.]

01° 30′ N

28° 20′ W

4/10 OVERCAST   VISIBILITY UNLIMITED

. SEA LIGHT   CAN YOU TELL PFX [Fernando
de Noronha] TO LISTEN FOR ME."

"Dit darr dit, dit darr dit [Received OK]. QSK
[What time will you call me again?]"

"QSK [I will call you again at] 12:45   MNI TKS
[Many thanks]," I sent out gratefully.

"OK   QSK   12:45 [Till 12:45]," came back
the friendly clicks from the radio towers on top
of the hill in Santiago.

That was really our good-by to the island. For
try as I might at twelve-forty-five, I never heard
him again.

CHAPTER XXXII

"ALL THE LAMPS ARE LIT"

I WOULD have to put out a CQ (General call), I thought in desperation, after another unsuccessful attempt at twelve-forty-five to contact Porto Praia. Perhaps some boat would answer me. I would sign it *Lindbergh Plane,* this time, instead of KHCAL. That might bring results. It sometimes worked. Stations apparently stone-deaf to KHCAL would speak up quickly to *Lindbergh Plane.* I only used this unprofessional signature as a last resort. I thought it a little unfair, somehow, not exactly sporting, like using live bait on your fishing-rod instead of a regulation fly.

But, now, I didn't care. The Pan American stations might, of course, be hearing me all the time, even though I couldn't hear them, but I wanted some kind of an answer, something tangible.

"CQ CQ [General call to all stations] LISTENING 28 TO 48 [meters] LINDBERGH PLANE."

"LINDBERGH LINDBERGH LINDBERGH," I hardly had the bait in the water before I got a bite!

"DDEA SS CAPARCONA BOUND RIO QRK [I receive you well. Your signals are good.]."

A ship, answering us—loud clear notes. Good, I had someone at last. They gave us their weather and position and then asked for ours.

"POSN 13:00 GMT [Eleven hours behind us: five more to go. Five hours was not as long as a flight from New York to St. Louis, I thought as I tapped.]

00° 15′ N

29° 25′ W

1/10 OVERCAST   VISIBILITY UNLIMITED

SEA LIGHT   WIND 10 KNOTS 135°   ALTI-

TUDE 800   COULD YOU RELAY LAST POSN TO

PVJ [Rio] OR PVB [Bahia]."

"OK," they answered, "WHERE BOUND?"

Where bound? Why, Natal, of course—BOUND NATAL. So indelibly stamped on my mind was our destination, it seemed surprising even to be asked the question. It had been our goal for weeks now. That half-forgotten ride down the coast of Africa, on the back of the wind; the long dusty wait at Santiago; the sultry trials at Bathurst; that fierce moonlit drive across the windless bay; the long night of work just behind us—it had all been to get to Natal.

The words, though, as I sent them over the radio, gave me an acute flash of excitement. They sounded clipped, sharp and swift, like the ping of an arrow, leaving its string. For today we were really bound for Natal like that, pointed at it, speeding towards it, like an arrow sprung from its bow: "BOUND NATAL."

The plane rocked gently. It was my husband moving the stick to attract my attention. I sat up quickly. What was it? His right hand pointed, out of the cockpit, to the north. There on the blue horizon was a ship! The first we had seen since those solitary lights below us in the dark off Bathurst, eleven hours before. A tiny speck only on the horizon, it was comforting as the first sight of land and bright as a beacon fire.

It is strange how the smallest touch of human life in the wilderness will light a landscape. Flying over the wastes of Arizona or New Mexico, I have noticed, even a deserted shack, a pile of stones hand-placed, or a patch of land once cultivated by man, shines out of the wilderness like a distant field in a ray of sunshine. It is lit with a strange brightness which is not explained by differences of color and light, but seems more to be a kind of warmth left there by the touch of humanity, a glowing ember of Promethean fire.

But this, the first ship on the South American side of the Atlantic, was more than an ember. It was a spark of life itself. It seemed the central point of an orbit, with the sky and sea rayed out from it in all directions. It lit the ocean like a lamp.

"POSN 14:00 GMT [Twelve hours behind us; only four to go.]

01° 00′ S [We had crossed the equator!]

30° 10′ W

COURSE 226° TRUE

MAKING 100 KNOTS   8/10 OVERCAST

VISIBILITY UNLIMITED."

"Unlimited"—we could see as far as a ship on the edge of the round ocean.

I looked up from the radio again. What were we doing now? We were going down. My husband was pointing at something straight ahead. I could not see from the back cockpit. Yes—there was another ship, this time right on our course, a freighter, steaming along slowly, pulling a white wake behind. We were fast catching up to her, now diving down, down, down. (What did they think of us coming out of the sky with no warning? Did we give them as much thrill as they gave us? A second ship! We must be well across the ocean, in the converging lanes to South America.) Now on top of her, the masts and smokestack came up to meet us. Roaring over her, for one second we were in her world. She there, we here; separated from each other by days of slow sea-travel but for this second together, sharing the time, the place. The blue star on her funnel, the

decks, the cargo, someone waving, we could see.
And on the side of the hull—yes—I could read
as we passed, her name, *Aldebaran*—(Aldebaran,
lovely star—a good omen!)

Up, up, up, we were climbing back into our
own world, our own time. The *Aldebaran* was
left behind, dropped back in the water, painfully
plodding along. Bound for South America, too,
how long would she take to get there? While *we*,
I thought, as we roared away—we would be at
Natal tonight, this afternoon even. Only four
hours to go.

"Arcturus, Aldebaran, Alpheratz," I repeated
reminiscently as we leveled out and straightened
our course again. Perhaps that first white speck
on the horizon was *Arcturus,* and the next ship
we passed would be *Alpheratz.*

The next ship, however, was not *Alpheratz.*
It was the *Westfalen,* the German catapult ship
stationed in the Atlantic for the transoceanic flying service. She had passed Fernando de Noronha,
that tiny island off the coast of Brazil, in the
morning, and lay almost on our course. We were
in contact with them (DDWE) for about two
hours, sending weather and position reports, and
transmitting on long wave for radio bearings.
They gave us our bearing from their ship, and

we turned slightly off course and headed in their direction.

"QRT [Stop sending]," the ship's operator broke off abruptly, "SEE YOU ON OUR PORT SIDE."

I looked out over the edge of the cockpit. There it was—a broad ship, steaming ahead of us, its plane, the catapult track, and the crooked arm of its derrick perched incongruously on top, looking like miniature toys from this height. We were diving down to meet them.

Suddenly I was aware of the men on deck, many bare arms waving, and steam puffing from a stack, visible sign of the blasts of salute we could not hear through the roar of our engine.

I held up my arm and waved frantically, conscious of that supreme thrill of communication. It is the most exciting thing in life anyway, whether you find it in a book or in conversation or in the understanding of two minds. But this, the momentary synthesis of two kinds of communication, was almost unbearable in its intensity. All night and all day I had been struggling to speak over a radio. I had been able to contact people only through my fingers, and my ears, like someone who is blind. But now, suddenly, I could see. A veil had dropped away. I could see, face to face. One of those men waving on deck was the radio operator I had been talking to. I raised my arm again—wonderful!

Now we were past. We were climbing up again, back to blind communication.

"MANY THANKS ALL HELP," I signaled back.

The operator on the *Westfalen* answered, giving us a bearing to Fernando de Noronha and to Natal. Then, "XMAS WISHES AND HAPPY NEW YEAR," he signed off, "FROM ALL ON DDWE." (Those bare arms waving from the deck.) "Xmas wishes"—on that tropical sea! I had never felt so far away from Christmas. But, of course, it was December, I recalled, December sixth. It was even possible that we might get home for Christmas. I let myself think about it; it was so near. "The men are sailing home from Troy," I thought, "And all the lamps are lit." The line jingled in my head as it always did when I was going home. It had danced to the rhythm of the train, coming back from school. It had throbbed in the engines of a steamer, coming into port. And now, again:

> The men are sailing home from Troy,
> And all the lamps are lit.[1]

I was very happy. We were only forty miles from Fernando de Noronha. The day was clear and cool. I did not feel sleepy at all. I could have gone on indefinitely, and the flight was almost over. We were coasting downhill, I felt, into Natal. Now over Fernando de Noronha, that bare little

---

[1] From "My Heart" by Elizabeth Madox Roberts.

island with one steep peak sticking up like a long French roll on end. Now bumping around its steep sides. Now off straight for Natal. Now in contact with the Pan American station at Ceara again.

"POSN 16:45 GMT [Almost fifteen hours behind us—an hour to go.]

04° 40′ s

33° 40′ w

CLEAR AND UNLIMITED   SEA LIGHT

WIND 15 KNOTS 60°."

Only an hour to go! An hour was nothing. An hour could be measured easily. As a child one had a nap of an hour, staring up at the flies counterpointing around the ceiling light. In school the classes were an hour, the squeak of chalk on a blackboard, the clock ticking in jumps, and the tantalizing smell of burning leaves coming in the window. It was an hour's drive from Englewood to New York. I would do it in my mind, every inch of the way, and then perhaps, by that time—

Down the driveway and around the curve— such a bad curve—go slow here. Past the entrance with the silver birches all leaning out to meet you, the corner of the big Brinkerhoff place, now deserted, windows gutted out, and a forest of young shoots where there used to be lawn. Up the hill—purr of the engine. The magnolia-trees-

place. Beech road and bicycle days. Past the
school, our old house, the chestnut tree, the elm
where the sand-box was. Up, up, past Woodland
Street where we used to ride. Pierce's pond where
we learned to skate, minute puddle with rustic
bridge we thought was the Hudson River. Up,
now past the Sunday-walk limit, to the cliffs. Slow
down, turn along the cliff road—foot down on the
accelerator—next—

My husband was wobbling the stick again. I
looked up. The first dim line of land was pushing
up over the horizon—South America. It did not
really give me as much thrill as the boats. It was
then I realized, for the first time, that we were on
the other side. As for South America—well, I expected it to appear—and there it was.

Nevertheless I gave up driving the car from
Englewood to New York and kept my eye on that
dim line, watching it harden from a stationary
cloud-rim to the fixed, irregular outline of a
shore.

> The men are sailing home from Troy,
> And all the lamps are lit

We would be there in no time. I turned back
to the radio; Ceara was calling again. They had
a message for us. I took it down. It was the one
we had received almost ten hours before from
Rio while we were still in the dark, on the other

side of the ocean. I passed it forward to my husband. How strange to read it again, now we were almost there:

"PAA BARGE AT NATAL [The coast of Brazil spread low and green in the slight haze ahead.] LOCATED ON RIVER [We came on it very quickly, following the coast for only a few minutes.] AT SOUTH WEST EDGE OF CITY STOP [There was Natal at last—that group of white houses running up a green hill, those palms on the skyline.] BETWEEN CITY AND LARGE AERO POSTALE HANGAR AND RAMP STOP [My husband looked back and signaled with his hand, 'Five minutes more.'] CAUTION TALL RADIO MASTS—[There they were, there was the hangar; we were circling!] FEW SPARE PARTS AVAILABLE ON BARGE [I could see it now, a square white barge on the river, flying an American flag.]"

We were spiraling down fast. I had hardly time to signal Ceara that we were landing. Quick, reel in the antenna before it hits the water. Fasten the brake, turn off the switches. Unplug the earphones. (At last! How sore my ears were from the pressure.) Now, fix up a little. Water on a handkerchief. Wipe my face. Comb my hair. Put on the helmet again and fasten the belt for landing.

Just in time. We were skimming over the surface of the water. The engine throttled, the propeller whirring idly, we were settling down gently like a gull coming to rest. There, we had clipped the water, riding along it with little slaps like a skipping stone. Now, sinking back in it. The rush of water over the pontoons as we slowed down. The surge forward as we came to a floating position. The blast of air as the plane started again, turning heavily, charging slowly through the water toward the barge. Creature of water again, now, no longer a bird of the air.

I took out my pad and, in the jolting motion of the waves, wrote unsteadily, "Landed Natal 17:55 GMT."

CHAPTER XXXIII

"AND SHUT OUR MINDS

TO THE SEA"

IT was suddenly very hot, stifling. The sun beat
down with oven-heat on the flat-roofed barge.
(It was three o'clock in Natal.) The desire to
sleep came over me in a warm wave. I was drunk
with it, light-headed.

We were taken quickly from the barge to shore
and, in a car, through blazing white streets, winding up a hill to a cool house overlooking the town.

Then I found we were climbing up a steep
slope to a bungalow, my feet unsteady as they
touched firm ground again and my thoughts in
a haze. I stubbed my shoe against little loose
stones and scuffed up dust as I plodded.

Still climbing up this hill, I thought vaguely,
my mind jumping back over an ocean and many
days, would we ever get . . . ? What hill? I
caught myself, waking up sharply. We had never
climbed this hill before. We were not at Porto
Praia, now, but in Brazil.

We came to the top and paused a moment to

look down over green roofs, and feather-duster palms flattened in the wind; over the brown streaked river, to the sea, blue and flecked with whitecaps.

Whitecaps, my mind leaped instinctively—why, there's a wind, a good wind!

A wind—I stopped myself, smiling—but we were not at Bathurst; we were at Natal. We no longer needed the wind.

APPENDIX

Compiled by C. A. L.

Our plane, the *Tingmissartoq*, was designed and constructed at Burbank, California, in 1929. We laid down general specifications to the effect that it must be a low-wing, full cantilever monoplane, with a radial air-cooled engine. It was the first plane of a type which became known as the "Lockheed Sirius." We ran acceptance tests in the winter and spring of 1930. In April of that year, the plane broke the transcontinental record, flying from California to New York in less than fifteen hours.

In 1931 the wheels were replaced with pontoons, a larger engine installed, and a flight was made over the Arctic route to the Orient.

In 1933 a third engine, with a controllable pitch propeller, was installed, and the plane equipped for a survey flight over the air-routes of the Atlantic. At the end of this flight it was placed, fully equipped, in the American Museum of Natural History, where it now hangs in the Hall of Ocean Life. Accounts of these flights have been published in the *National Geographic Magazine*, September, 1934, and in *North to the Orient*, Harcourt, Brace and Company, 1935.

The description of the plane and equipment in the following pages is for the Europe to South America section of the Atlantic survey flight in 1933. The articles which were removed for the take-off from Bathurst, for the flight across the Atlantic to South America, are marked with an asterisk.

> Plane—Lockheed Sirius
> Engine—Wright Cyclone F (710 H.P.)
> Pontoons—Edo
> Propeller—Hamilton controllable pitch

INSTRUMENTS

Directional gyro—Sperry
Gyroscopic horizon—Sperry
Turn and bank indicator—Pioneer
Vacuum gauge for gyroscopes—Pioneer
Aperiodic compass—Ritchie
Aperiodic compass—Pioneer
Altimeter—Pioneer
Rate of climb indicator—Pioneer
Air speed indicator—Pioneer
Ice indicator—Motometer
Tachometer—Pioneer
Fuel quantity gauge—Pioneer
Fuel pressure gauge—Pioneer
Oil pressure gauge—Pioneer
Oil temperature gauge—Pioneer
Cylinder temperature gauge—General Electric
Manifold pressure gauge—Pioneer
Volt-ammeter—Weston

PLANE'S RADIO EQUIPMENT

Pan American Airways standard type 10C-2 transmitter, rated at 12 watts CW telegraph, adjustable on the following frequencies:

Frequency kilocycles	Wave-length meters	Normal day range miles	Normal night range miles
333	900	0-50	0-200
500	600	0-75	0-200
3115	96.3	0-150	0-300
5515	54.3	0-300	300-1200
8340	35.9	0-450	300-2200
12480	24.6	0-600	400-3500

Weight of transmitter complete with one set of coils.. 12 lbs. 0 oz.
5 extra sets of coils covering additional frequencies.... 7 lbs. 8 oz.

Pan American Airways standard type ACC receiver, covering the following frequency bands:

Frequency kilocycles	Wave-length meters
577 to 315	520 to 950
23440 to 1725	12.8 to 260

Weight of receiver, complete with all coils...... 11 lbs. 4 oz.
B battery .... 9 lbs. 0 oz.

THE TINGMISSARTOQ in the Hall of Ocean Life, American Museum of Natural History, where it was placed on its return from the Atlantic survey flights in 1933.

Antenna reel and trailing wire, complete with
ball-weight .... 5 lbs. 10 oz.
Direction finder (fixed loop antenna inside of
fuselage)
Dynamotor—HA-3 .... 16 lbs. 12 oz.
Storage battery (plane's storage battery also used
for operating radio)
*1 spare part box............................. 2 lbs. 15 oz.
7 vacuum tubes .... 1 lb. 7 oz.
2 testing wires .... 2½ oz.
roll repair tape .... ½ oz.
*1 ball antenna weight .... 1 lb. 10 oz.
1 long antenna weight .... 8½ oz.
1 coil wire solder, 1 coil wire.................. 11 oz.
1 box fuses .... 1 oz.
3 light bulbs .... 1 oz.
*1 list "Stations Performing Special Services" in-
cluding Supplement No. 16 .... 1 lb. 2½ oz.
*1 list "Fixed and Land Stations"................ 1 lb. 6 oz.
*1 supplement to list "Fixed and Land Stations".. 6 oz.
*1 copy "Radio Aids to Navigation".............. 1 lb. 2 oz.
radio licenses .... 1 oz.
message pad .... 10 oz.
pencils, clips, and rubber bands (listed under
Navigation Equipment)
flashlights (listed under Navigation Equipment)

EMERGENCY RADIO EQUIPMENT

Watertight and padded aluminum box, containing transmitter, receiver, batteries, antenna, earphones, extra vacuum tubes, and all equipment necessary for operation, independent of plane's regular radio.

Transmitter, adjustable on the following frequencies:

Frequency kilocycles	Wave-length meters	Normal day range miles	Normal night range miles
5515	54.3	0-300	300-1200
8340	35.9	0-450	300-2200

Receiver, covering the following frequency bands:

Frequency kilocycles	Wave-length meters
555 to 320	540 to 930
11110 to 4615	27 to 65

During its tests, the emergency radio was dropped 18 feet, onto a concrete floor. It was then set up and communication established with a station 350 miles away, in daylight. It was also submerged in water for 24 hours, and tested again when brought to the surface.

Weight of emergency radio complete...... 44 lbs. 0 oz.

The radio equipment was designed, constructed, and tested under the supervision of Mr. Hugo Leuteritz, Chief Communication Engineer of Pan American Airways. Mr. Leuteritz also had charge of arrangements for our schedules with the Pan American stations in South America.

AIRPLANE AND ENGINE EQUIPMENT

*1 anchor, linen rope, and chain	37 lbs. 0	oz.
*1 anchor bridle rope	8 lbs. 8	oz.
1 canvas anchor bag (to be filled with sand or rocks)	1 lb. 13	oz.
1 sea anchor	4 lbs. 6	oz.
2 linen wing ropes	6 lbs. 4	oz.
*2 shackles for wing ropes	4	oz.
*1 kerosene mooring lantern	1 lb. 13	oz.
*1 extra wick for mooring lantern	½	oz.
*1 canteen for kerosene (for mooring lantern)	8½	oz.
*kerosene for mooring lantern	12	oz.
1 bilge pump	2 lbs. 8	oz.
1 bilge pump hose	2 lbs. 2	oz.
*1 gasoline and oil funnel	2 lbs. 12	oz.
1 felt gasoline strainer	5	oz.
*1 felt gasoline strainer	5	oz.
*1 aluminum pail	2 lbs. 0	oz.
*1 pontoon gasoline tank measure	3	oz.
*3 cans tetraethyl lead	16 lbs. 11	oz.
*1 measure for tetraethyl lead	4	oz.
1 pr. rubber gloves (tetraethyl lead)	2½	oz.
1 fire extinguisher	3 lbs. 15	oz.
2 air cushions for seats	3 lbs. 6	oz.
*1 can dope	1 lb. 6	oz.
*1 dope brush	2	oz.
*linen strips for wing repairs	5	oz.
*1 can pontoon cement	3 lbs. 4	oz.
*1 can black paint	5	oz.
*1 paint brush	2	oz.
*1 pontoon hand hole cover	8	oz.
1 pontoon hand hole rubber gasket	½	oz.
*1 sheet duralumin	4 lbs. 0	oz.
*1 file for sheet duralumin	7	oz.
*1 box sheet metal screws	9	oz.
1 bag duralumin rivets, cotter keys, bolts, nuts, and washers	1 lb. 0	oz.

APPENDIX 267

* 1 hand drill	1 lb.	8	oz.
*assorted drills		3	oz.
1 hatchet (with hammer head)	1 lb.	5½	oz.
* 1 engine hand crank	2 lbs.	12	oz.
1 box fuses		1½	oz.
1 coil safety wire		6	oz.
* 1 hydrometer		4	oz.
* 1 insect spray gun		9	oz.
* 1 can spray fluid		10	oz.
1 roll adhesive tape		5	oz.
* 1 can light oil		6	oz.
* 1 engine and accessory manual (parts deleted)		9	oz.
1 tool bag		6	oz.
1 adjustable open end wrench, 8"		7	oz.
* 1 small adjustable wrench		2	oz.
1 pliers, small size		2	oz.
1 pliers, medium size		4	oz.
1 file, 6"		1	oz.
1 cold chisel		1	oz.
1 screwdriver, 4"		4	oz.
4 hack saw blades		3	oz.
sandpaper		½	oz.
1 spark plug wrench		6	oz.
1 spark plug wrench handle		4	oz.
*spark plug gap adjusting tool		11	oz.
1 magneto point wrench		½	oz.
1 stone for magneto points		½	oz.
1 valve adjusting wrench		6	oz.
* 1 valve spring compressor	1 lb.	4	oz.
1 valve clearance gauge		1	oz.
* 1 feeler gauge set		4	oz.
* 1 push rod adjusting nut wrench		1½	oz.
* 1 carburetor jet wrench		4	oz.
* 1 end wrench, ½"		3	oz.
* 1 box wrench, ⅜" & ⁷⁄₁₆"		2	oz.
* 1 box wrench, ½"		3	oz.
* 1 box wrench, ½" & ⁹⁄₁₆"		3	oz.
* 2 box wrenches, ⅝" & ¹¹⁄₁₆"		12	oz.
* 1 box wrench, ¾"		9	oz.
* 1 box wrench, 1⅛"		13	oz.
* 1 wrench handle		10	oz.
* 1 Allen wrench, ¼"		1	oz.
* 1 Allen wrench, ³⁄₁₆"		1	oz.
* 1 Allen wrench, ⁵⁄₁₆"		2	oz.
* 1 open end wrench, ½" & ⁷⁄₁₆"		3	oz.
* 1 open end wrench, ⅝" & ⁹⁄₁₆"		4	oz.
* 1 open end wrench, 1" & ¾"		7	oz.
* 1 open end wrench, 1⁵⁄₁₆"		9	oz.
* 1 intake crowfoot lug wrench		6	oz.
* 1 wrench extension	1 lb.	1	oz.

```
*1  crowfoot wrench, ⅝" ..........................          3   oz.
*1  propeller wrench ...........................   3 lbs.  0   oz.
*1  propeller wrench, inner ....................   3 lbs.  2   oz.
*1  grease gun ..................................   1 lb.  1   oz.
*1  oil gun .....................................         13   oz.
 2  spark plugs .................................          5   oz.
*7  spark plugs .................................         15   oz.
              Total   weight  ........................ 138 lbs.  7   oz.
```

NAVIGATION EQUIPMENT

```
 1  sextant and box ............................   4 lbs. 12   oz.
 1  hour angle chronometer .....................          4   oz.
 1  extra chronometer ..........................          5   oz.
 1  aluminum jar for carrying chronometers ......         3½ oz.
*1  eight day chronometer ......................   1 lb.  3   oz.
 1  protractor .................................          ½ oz.
 1  slide rule .................................          1   oz.
*1  dividers ...................................          1   oz.
 1  Air Almanac for 1933 .......................         12   oz.
 1  Weems Line of Position Book ................          7   oz.
 1  looseleaf notebook and paper ...............   1 lb.  8   oz.
calculation sheets ............................          1½ oz.
 6  pencils ....................................          1   oz.
rubber bands and clips ........................          1   oz.
 1  battery flashlight (5-cell) ................   1 lb. 11½ oz.
 1  hand generator flashlight ..................          7½ oz.
 3  extra flashlight bulbs .....................          1   oz.
*1  rubberized silk globe of the world .........          2½ oz.
 1  Mercator's chart of the Atlantic Ocean, 3
       sections ...................................        10   oz.
*1  Great Circle sailing chart of the Atlantic Ocean     4   oz.
*2  U. S. monthly pilot charts (October and Novem-
       ber, 1933) .................................         3   oz.
*2  British monthly pilot charts (October and
       November, 1933) ............................         3   oz.
*1  magnetic variation chart for Europe ..........         1   oz.
*1  map of Spain and Portugal ....................         2   oz.
*2  Portuguese weather maps ......................         1   oz.
*3  detailed charts of the Azores ................        10   oz.
*1  map of Madeira ...............................         2   oz.
*1  detailed chart of Funchal, Madeira ...........         1   oz.
 2  charts of the Cape Verde Islands ...........          8   oz.
*1  chart—Cape Glir to Garnet Head, including
       Canaries ...................................         5   oz.
 1  map of Africa ..............................          1   oz.
              Total  weight  ......................... 15 lbs.  6   oz.
```

PERSONAL FLYING EQUIPMENT

1 parka coat (C. A. L.) .... 4 lbs. 1 oz.
*1 hood for parka coat (C. A. L.) .... 6½ oz.
1 parka coat (A. M. L.) .... 3 lbs. 3 oz.
1 hood for parka coat (A. M. L.) .... 6 oz.
2 fur-lined helmets .... 14 oz.
2 cloth helmets .... 6 oz.
2 pr. goggles .... 8 oz.
2 pr. mittens (wool-lined) .... 10 oz.
1 pr. kamiks, sealskin and dogskin lined (Eskimo
    boots) (A. M. L.) .... 2 lbs. 3 oz.
*1 pr. kamiks, sealskin and dogskin lined (C. A. L.) 3 lbs. 4 oz.
*1 pr. rubber boots (C. A. L.) .... 5 lbs. 7 oz.
*1 pr. rubber boots (A. M. L.) .... 4 lbs. 11½ oz.
*1 pr. extra boot laces .... ½ oz.
4 pr. heavy wool socks .... 1 lb. 10 oz.
1 southwester hat and suit (C. A. L.) .... 3 lbs. 5 oz.
1 southwester hat and suit (A. M. L.) .... 3 lbs. 3½ oz.
1 pr. amber glasses (for eye protection against
    glare) .... 1 oz.
ear cotton .... ½ oz.
*2 life preservers (inflatable type) .... 2 lbs. 11 oz.
personal clothing worn while flying (A. M. L.).... 3 lbs. 2 oz.
personal clothing worn while flying (C. A. L.)..... 5 lbs. 10 oz.
flashlights (listed under Navigation Equipment)
knife (listed under Emergency Equipment for
    Forced Landing on Land)
            Total weight .... 45 lbs. 11½ oz.

PERSONAL EQUIPMENT

*personal clothing and equipment (18 lbs. each)... 36 lbs. 0 oz.

*All except 12 ounces of personal equipment was removed from
the plane for the take-off from Bathurst.*

PARACHUTE EQUIPMENT

No parachutes were carried because most of the flying was over
the ocean, or over territory where survival would depend upon
having the emergency equipment which was carried in the plane.
Greater safety could be obtained by transferring the weight of
parachutes into additional food and water.

PHOTOGRAPHIC EQUIPMENT

*1 camera with 50 mm. lens (35 mm. film)........ 1 lb. 4 oz.
*1 case and shoulder-strap for camera .... 7 oz.

*1 sunshade ....   1 oz.
*1 filter ....   ½ oz.
*6 film magazines and aluminum containers (35
    exposures each) ....   15 oz.
        Total weight ....   2 lbs. 11½ oz.

EMERGENCY EQUIPMENT FOR FORCED LANDING ON LAND

*1 tent (cloth floor and net door and window).....   6 lbs. 4 oz.
*1 sleeping bag (wool) ....   6 lbs. 0 oz.
 1 waterproof match box and matches ....   1½ oz.
 1 aluminum jar containing safety matches ....   5 oz.
 1 compass ....   1½ oz.
  maps (listed under Navigation Equipment)
 1 revolver (.38 caliber) ....   1 lb. 15 oz.
 6 rounds .38 cal. special ammunition ....   3½ oz.
*14 rounds .38 cal. special ammunition ....   8 oz.
 5 rounds .38 cal. tear gas shells ....   2 oz.
*1 revolver (.22 caliber) ....   1 lb. 7 oz.
*100 rounds .22 cal. long ammunition............   12 oz.
*50 rounds .22 cal. short ammunition............   4½ oz.
*1 can gun oil ....   3 oz.
  heavy fishline ....   14 oz.
  light fishline ....   1½ oz.
27 fishhooks (assorted sizes) ....   1 oz.
13 fishline swivels (assorted sizes) ....   1 oz.
  sinkers (to be obtained from engine—nuts, bolts,
    etc.)
 1 fish net (about 25 ft. long) ....   7 oz.
 1 mosquito net ....   6 oz.
 2 mosquito headnets ....   3½ oz.
 2 bottles citronella oil ....   12 oz.
 2 sun helmets ....   1 lb. 9½ oz.
  southwesters (listed under Personal Flying Equip-
    ment)
  parka coats (listed under Personal Flying Equip-
    ment)
  mittens (listed under Personal Flying Equipment)
 2 suits heavy wool underwear ....   3 lbs. 2 oz.
  other clothing (listed under Personal Flying
    Equipment)
  heavy thread ....   ½ oz.
 1 package of needles ....   ½ oz.
 1 coil flexible wire (for snares, etc.) ....   2 oz.
 1 pocket knife containing large blade, screwdriver,
    bottle opener, and awl ....   4 oz.
 1 aluminum pot and lid ....   3 oz.

1 first aid kit (containing various medicines, bandages, etc.) .... 2 lbs. 8 oz.
1 surgical kit (containing scissors, 2 forceps, thermometer, scalpel, needles, bottle of twisted silk, and lance with potassium permanganate crystals) 5 oz.
1 medical and first aid handbook (without binding) .... 3 oz.
ropes (listed under Airplane and Engine Equipment—wing ropes)
flashlights (listed under Navigation Equipment)
hatchet (listed under Airplane and Engine Equipment)
portable radio set (listed under Emergency Radio Equipment)
water canteens (listed under Emergency Provisions)
food (listed under Emergency Provisions)
Total weight .... 29 lbs. 6½ oz.

EMERGENCY EQUIPMENT FOR FORCED LANDING AT SEA

1 rubber boat .... 26 lbs. 1 oz.
1 rubber storm top .... 4 lbs. 5 oz.
mast, boom, sail, and bottom board .... 7 lbs. 15 oz.
1 pr. oars .... 3 lbs. 7½ oz.
2 air pumps ....: ... 2 lbs. 8 oz.
rubber patch sheet and tube of rubber cement.... 3½ oz.
bridle for sea anchor (listed under Airplane and Engine Equipment)
ropes (listed under Airplane and Engine Equipment—wing ropes)
2 Armburst cups .... 1 lb. 1½ oz.
1 Very pistol .... 1 lb. 8 oz.
10 Very pistol shells .... 1 lb. 15 oz.
sea anchor (listed under Airplane and Engine Equipment)
southwester hats and suits (listed under Personal Flying Equipment)
clothing (listed under Personal Flying Equipment, and Emergency Equipment for Forced Landing on Land)
hatchet (listed under Airplane and Engine Equipment)
heavy cord (listed under Emergency Equipment for Forced Landing on Land—heavy fishline)
flashlights (listed under Navigation Equipment)
food and water (listed under Emergency Provisions)
radio (listed under Emergency Radio Equipment)

sextant, chronometer, and other navigation equipment (listed under Navigation Equipment)

Total weight .... 49 lbs.   ½ oz.

EMERGENCY PROVISIONS

3 water canteens (2 gallons each)	9 lbs.	4	oz.
2 water canteens (1 gallon each)	4 lbs.	0	oz.
8 gallons water	67 lbs.	0	oz.
2 tins biscuits	22 lbs.	2½	oz.
*1 can biscuits	1 lb.	6	oz.
*2 cans butter	2 lbs.	6	oz.
*23 cans composition emergency rations	17 lbs.	5	oz.
4 cans composition emergency rations	3 lbs.	0	oz.
*4 cans corned beef	3 lbs.	15	oz.
*1 can fish	1 lb.	3	oz.
*2 cans baked beans	1 lb.	11	oz.
8 cans baked beans	6 lbs.	12½	oz.
9 cans tomatoes	8 lbs.	9	oz.
*3 cans tomatoes	2 lbs.	14	oz.
6 packages dried figs	3 lbs.	6	oz.
*2 packages containing tins of malted milk tablets	11 lbs.	1	oz.
*2 cans bouillon cubes		5½	oz.
*1 can powdered milk	1 lb.	5	oz.
*3 packages dried soup		12½	oz.
1 canvas food bag	1 lb.	8	oz.
*1 canvas food bag	2 lbs.	4	oz.
1 can opener (listed under Emergency Equipment for Forced Landing on Land)			
Total weight	172 lbs.	2	oz.

LOG OF ATLANTIC SURVEY FLIGHT: 1933

Greenwich Mean Time is used throughout this log (measured from Greenwich mean midnight)

July 9	19:37	Took off Flushing Bay, Long Island, New York.
	22:38	Landed South Pond, Maine.
July 10		Took off South Pond, Maine.
		Landed North Haven, Maine.
		(Flying time—20 minutes)
July 11	19:12	Took off North Haven, Maine.
	21:49	Landed Halifax, Nova Scotia.
July 12	15:13	Took off Halifax, Nova Scotia.
	20:44	Landed St. John's, Newfoundland.
July 14	13:08	Took off St. John's, Newfoundland.
	20:57	Landed Cartwright, Labrador.

July 17	17:48	Took off Cartwright, Labrador.
	19:41	Landed Carters Basin, Labrador.
	20:11	Took off Carters Basin, Labrador.
	21:15	Landed Cartwright, Labrador.
July 21	14:22	Took off Cartwright, Labrador.
	17:00	Landed Hopedale, Labrador.
	20:12	Took off Hopedale, Labrador.
	22:21	Landed Hebron, Labrador.
July 22	16:02	Took off Hebron, Labrador.
	22:22	Landed Godthaab, Greenland.
July 25	17:28	Took off Godthaab, Greenland.
	20:30	Landed Eskimo village, Greenland.
	20:50	Took off Eskimo village, Greenland.
	21:10	Landed Holsteinsborg, Greenland.
July 30	15:03	Took off Holsteinsborg, Greenland.
	20:08	Landed Holsteinsborg, Greenland.
August 3	13:21	Took off Holsteinsborg, Greenland.
	17:15	Landed Holsteinsborg, Greenland.
August 4	14:42	Took off Holsteinsborg, Greenland.
	22:00	Landed Ella Island, Greenland.
August 5	10:46	Took off Ella Island, Greenland.
	12:10	Landed Eskimonaes, Greenland.
August 6	12:05	Took off Eskimonaes, Greenland.
	20:18	Landed Angmagssalik, Greenland.
August 8	15:08	Took off Angmagssalik, Greenland.
	19:27	Landed Godthaab, Greenland.
	21:12	Took off Godthaab, Greenland.
	23:42	Landed Julianehaab, Greenland.
August 12	14:42	Took off Julianehaab, Greenland.
	19:33	Landed Angmagssalik, Greenland.
August 15	15:27	Took off Angmagssalik, Greenland.
	20:44	Landed Videy, Iceland.
August 17		Took off Videy, Iceland.
		Landed Reykjavik, Iceland.
		(Flying time—15 minutes)
August 22	12:16	Took off Reykjavik, Iceland.
	18:02	Landed Eskifjordur, Iceland.
August 23	12:53	Took off Eskifjordur, Iceland.
	15:55	Landed Tvera, Faeroe Islands.
August 24	12:31	Took off Tvera, Faeroe Islands.
	15:03	Landed Lerwick, Shetland Islands.
August 26	11:17	Took off Lerwick, Shetland Islands.
	16:18	Landed Copenhagen, Denmark.
September 3	10:16	Took off Copenhagen, Denmark.
	14:12	Landed Stockholm, Sweden.

September 17	12:29	Took off Stockholm, Sweden.
	14:21	Landed Karlskrona, Sweden.
September 20	11:11	Took off Karlskrona, Sweden.
	16:21	Landed Helsingfors, Finland.
September 22	09:10	Took off Helsingfors, Finland.
	11:00	Landed Leningrad, Russia.
September 25	11:22	Took off Leningrad, Russia.
	14:51	Landed Moscow, Russia.
September 29	08:43	Took off Moscow, Russia.
	13:06	Landed Tallinn, Estonia.
October 1	10:10	Took off Tallinn, Estonia.
	14:45	Landed Oslo, Norway.
October 3	11:17	Took off Oslo, Norway.
	14:03	Landed Stavanger, Norway.
October 4	10:00	Took off Stavanger, Norway.
	15:43	Landed Southampton, England.
October 23	11:26	Took off Southampton, England.
	16:45	Landed Galway, Ireland.
October 25	11:23	Took off Galway, Ireland.
	15:21	Landed Inverness, Scotland.
October 26	13:12	Took off Inverness, Scotland.
	17:23	Landed Les Mureaux, France.
November 2	12:16	Took off Les Mureaux, France.
	14:49	Landed Amsterdam, Holland.
November 7	11:29	Took off Amsterdam, Holland.
	15:55	Landed Rotterdam, Holland.
November 8	11:38	Took off Rotterdam, Holland.
	14:50	Landed Geneva, Switzerland.
November 11	11:05	Took off Geneva, Switzerland.
	16:14	Landed Santona, Spain.
November 13	10:47	Took off Santona, Spain.
	14:29	Landed Rio Minho, Portugal.
November 15	10:49	Took off Rio Minho, Portugal.
	12:49	Landed Lisbon, Portugal.
November 21	07:08	Took off Lisbon, Portugal.
	16:25	Landed Horta, Azores.
November 23	14:44	Took off Horta, Azores.
	16:17	Landed Ponta Delgada, Azores.
November 24	09:01	Took off Ponta Delgada, Azores.
	15:57	Landed Las Palmas, Canary Islands.
November 26	08:40	Took off Las Palmas, Canary Islands.
	11:20	Landed Villa Cisneros, Rio de Oro.
November 27	08:48	Took off Villa Cisneros, Rio de Oro.
	15:01	Landed Santiago, Cape Verde Islands.

November 30	09:28	Took off Santiago, Cape Verde Islands.
	13:58	Landed Bathurst, Gambia.
December 6	02:00	Took off Bathurst, Gambia.
	17:55	Landed Natal, Brazil.
December 8	11:09	Took off Natal, Brazil.
	18:30	Landed Para, Brazil.
December 10	11:53	Took off Para, Brazil.
	19:31	Landed Manaos, Brazil.
December 12	09:48	Took off Manaos, Brazil.
	19:25	Landed Port-of-Spain, Trinidad.
December 14	12:59	Took off Port-of-Spain, Trinidad.
	18:32	Landed San Juan, Puerto Rico.
December 15	13:58	Took off San Juan, Puerto Rico.
	15:35	Landed San Pedro de Macoris, Santo Domingo
December 16	11:31	Took off San Pedro de Macoris, Santo Domingo.
	18:20	Landed Miami, Florida.
December 18	14:51	Took off Miami, Florida.
	19:23	Landed Charleston, South Carolina.
December 19	13:42	Took off Charleston, South Carolina.
	19:37	Landed Flushing Bay, Long Island, New York.